Atlas of the Bible Lands

Edited by

Harry Thomas Frank
Late Professor of Religion, Oberlin College

Consultant for Revised Edition
Roger S. Boraas
Professor of Religion, Upsala College

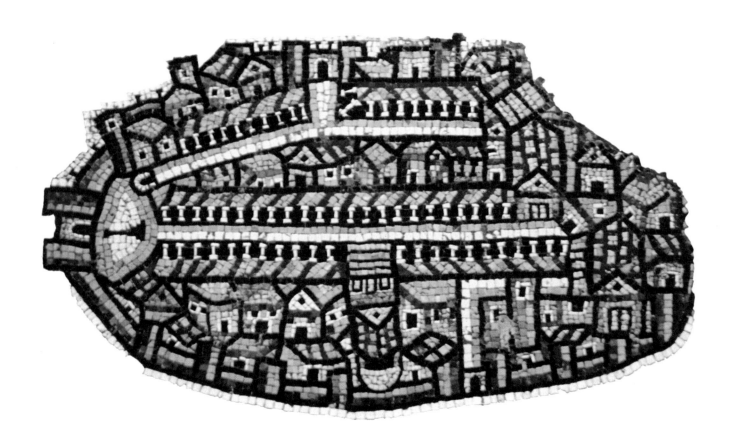

HAMMOND INCORPORATED   MAPLEWOOD, NEW JERSEY

Title Page illustration:
Detail of Jerusalem from the Medeba
mosaic map. The Damascus Gate is at
the far left. The mosaic dates from about
A.D. 560 and is the oldest map of the
Holy Land.

Wall painting from tomb at **Beni-hasan**
depicts Asian people, probably Amorites,
entering Egypt about 1900 B.C.

ATLAS OF THE BIBLE LANDS, *Revised Edition*
Entire contents © Copyright 1990, 1984, 1977
Revised 1997 by HAMMOND INCORPORATED
*All rights reserved. No part of this book may
be reproduced or utilized in any form or by any
means, electronic or mechanical including photo-
copying, recording or by any information storage
and retrieval system, without permission in writing
from the publisher.*

*The maps "Routes in Palestine" and "Economy of
Palestine" on pages 5 and 7 were prepared especially for
Abingdon Press and published in* The Interpreter's
Dictionary of the Bible, Supplementary Volume. *They are
reproduced here with Abingdon's permission.*

Library of Congress Cataloging-in-Publication Data

Hammond Incorporated.
    Atlas of the Bible Lands.

    Includes index.
        1. Bible—Geography—Maps.   I. Frank, Harry Thomas.
II. Boraas, Roger S.   III. Title.
G2230.H3   1990   220.9'1   89-675129
ISBN 0-8437-7056-2 case bound edition
ISBN 0-8437-7055-4 soft cover edition
Printed in the United States of America

Contents

Preface to the Revised Edition

THE BIBLE speaks to every human being. For believers —Jewish, Christian or Muslim—it sets the basic perceptions of God, human life, history, and meaning. Its ideas and images have permeated art, music and philosophy to become fundamental to any modern view of human wisdom, whether in support of or challenge to current ideas. So it belongs to and affects all humans.

The Bible is also a very specific, down-to-earth book. Like all of us it is rooted in time and place. This is part of its strength. It reaches people where they are—in this world, of this time. Unlike many speculative religions, which project worlds and meanings from emotions or spectacular imaginations, the Bible deals with folks who are born, learn, work, fight, marry, rejoice, weep, struggle and die. It declares the meaning of our shared life, our common experience, our present dangers, our hopes, our sense of purpose. In that it is God's Word to people.

So, through the Bible we follow Moses to Mt. Sinai (Exodus 19). We hear Deborah's victory song at Taanach (Judges 5). We see David dance on the way to Jerusalem (2 Samuel 6). We find Jeremiah wondering if God has abandoned him (Jeremiah 15). We hear the anguish of defeated Judeans in exile in Babylon (Psalm 137). We accompany Nehemiah on his evening inspection of the ramparts and gates of Jersualem (Nehemiah 2:11). We rejoice with Simeon at the birth of a new baby boy (Luke 2:22-32). We hear Jesus' stories about the Kingdom of God (Luke 15). We walk with a man down 4,000 feet in 18 miles from Jerusalem to Jericho and see him mugged on the road (Luke 10:30). We struggle with Paul on the way from Jerusalem to Damascus (Acts 9) and endure with him the storm and ship damage off Crete (Acts 27). In such matters the Bible speaks to us of events and meaning in specific places and times no matter where or when we live.

However, the times are remote (two or three thousand years ago), and the places are unfamiliar, frequently having strange names (Ur, Mizpah, the Kishon or Jabbok rivers). Having a realistic sense of those Biblical places helps sharpen our awareness of what the Bible says. Why would Abraham leave Ur or Haran and move to Shechem? Why did Israelites avoid the easy coast road in leaving Egypt at the Exodus? Why did David pick Jerusalem for the capital of his new kingdom? Geography, history and the sense of God's will are entwined closely in the Bible. Revelation of God's promises and warnings came to people through experiences in particular places at particular moments. Later reflections recall that meaning, sometimes embraced in recollections of the places and specific mention of the times.

With the help of this newly revised *Hammond's Atlas of the Bible Lands* the places may be found on easily readable up-to-date maps. The settings of the stories are richly illustrated. Maps, plans and photos combine to bring to the reader an immediate perception of the places in which the significant events occurred. The organization by time periods is aided by charts showing what happened in different parts of the Biblical world at the same time. They set the Biblical story against the backdrop of contemporary political developments. All this helps us follow the Biblical story from the earliest ancestors of Israel through the founding of the churches of the second century A.D. It reminds us that the places of knowing God are the places of earth, of our ordinary life.

R.S.B.

Upsala College, June 1989

...the land which you are going over to possess is a land of hills and valleys, which drinks water by the rain from heaven, a land which the Lord your God cares for; the eyes of the Lord your God are always upon it, from the beginning of the year to the end of the year.
—Deuteronomy 11:11-12

How to use this Atlas

Arrangement

This Atlas begins with an introductory section on the unique geography of the Holy Land. Besides terrain, vegetation and climate information, there are maps on trade routes and the economy of Palestine. The main collection of maps is arranged chronologically using the Biblical record from the Old and New Testament with a focus primarily on Palestine. The viewpoint broadens at appropriate intervals, to include the larger areas of the Ancient Near East and Greek and Roman worlds. These maps show important political changes, the course of empires and the expansion of the early Christian Church.

Also of special interest in the main collection of maps are the detailed plans of the Holy City of Jerusalem at critical points in Biblical history as well as reconstructions of other cities, ancient sites, battles and even buildings.

The last section of the Atlas brings the reader into the present with an essential look at the lands of the bible in modern times, along with an up-to-date map of major archaeological sites in Israel and Jordan. The time charts and the gazetteer-index at the back of the book are valuable reference tools for locating events in both time and place.

Place-names

The spellings of Biblical sites and geographical names used in the maps and index are those found in the Revised Standard Version (RSV) of the Bible. Alternative Biblical or other ancient names are placed in parentheses. A question mark following a site name indicates the location is possible or probable but not yet certain.

Names of political regions, empires, kingdoms and provinces are shown in large boldface capitals, e.g. **BABYLONIA**.

Names of tribal and ethnic groups are usually in lighter typeface, e.g. ARAMEANS.

Cities and towns are in lower case roman type, e.g. Tyre.

Seas, lakes, rivers, etc. are in lower case italic, e.g. *The Great Sea*, with later or modern place names in parentheses, e.g. *(Mediterranean Sea)*.

Mountain ranges are shown in italic capitals, e.g. *CAUCASUS*; mountain peaks are in lower case italics, e.g. *Mt. Tabor*.

Physical Map of Palestine

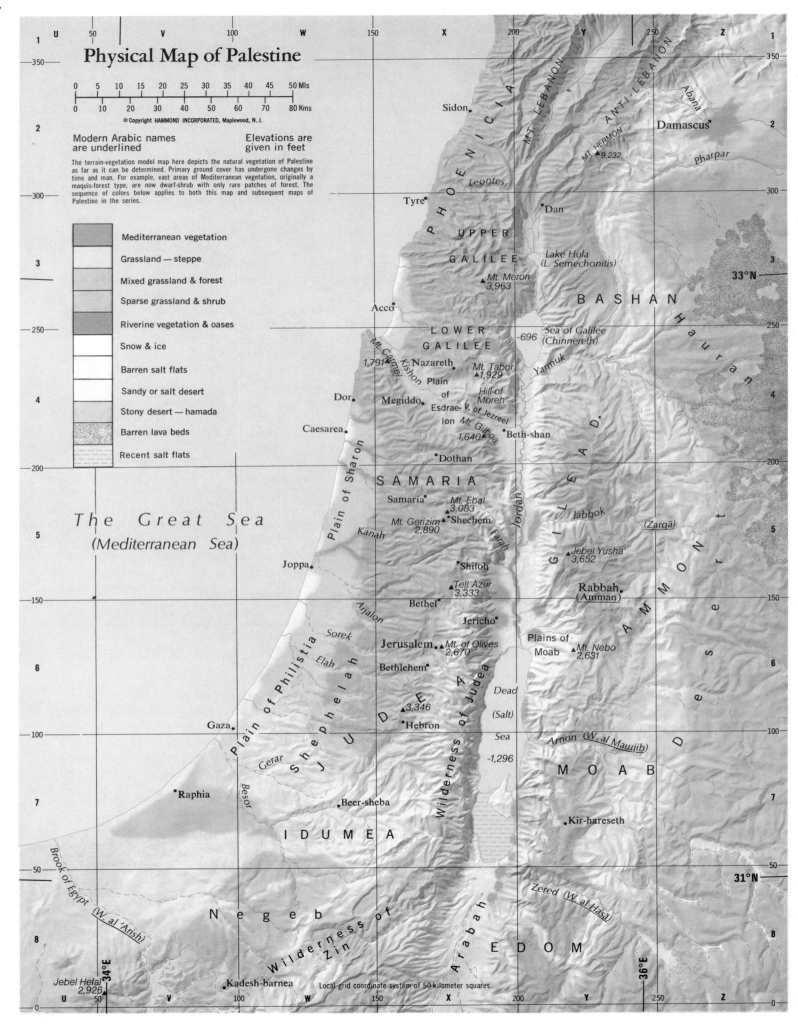

© Copyright HAMMOND INCORPORATED, Maplewood, N. J.

Modern Arabic names are underlined

Elevations are given in feet

The terrain-vegetation model map here depicts the natural vegetation of Palestine as far as it can be determined. Primary ground cover has undergone changes by time and man. For example, vast areas of Mediterranean vegetation, originally a maquis-forest type, are now dwarf-shrub with only rare patches of forest. The sequence of colors below applies to both this map and subsequent maps of Palestine in the series.

- Mediterranean vegetation
- Grassland — steppe
- Mixed grassland & forest
- Sparse grassland & shrub
- Riverine vegetation & oases
- Snow & ice
- Barren salt flats
- Sandy or salt desert
- Stony desert — hamada
- Barren lava beds
- Recent salt flats

The Great Sea
(Mediterranean Sea)

PHOENICIA

MT. LEBANON

ANTI-LEBANON

Abana

Sidon

Damascus

Pharpar

Leontes

MT. HERMON
9,232

Tyre

Dan

UPPER GALILEE

Lake Hula
(L. Semechonitis)

33°N

BASHAN

Acco

LOWER GALILEE

Sea of Galilee
(Chinnereth)

-696

Hauran

Mt. Meron
3,963

Mt. Carmel
1,791

Kishon

Nazareth

Mt. Tabor
1,929

Yarmuk

Plain of Esdraelon

Hill of Moreh

V. of Jezreel

Dor

Megiddo

Mt. Gilboa
1,640

Beth-shan

G I L E A D

Caesarea

Dothan

Plain of Sharon

SAMARIA

Samaria

Mt. Ebal
3,083

Jordan

Farah

Jabbok

(Zarqā)

Mt. Gerizim
2,890

Shechem

Kanah

Jebel Yusha
3,652

Shiloh

Tell Azur
3,333

Joppa

Rabbah
(Amman)

A M M O N

Bethel

Ajalon

Jericho

Sorek

Plains of Moab

Elah

Jerusalem

Mt. of Olives
2,670

Mt. Nebo
2,631

Shephelah

Bethlehem

D e s e r t

Gaza

J U D E A

Wilderness of Judea

Dead
(Salt)
Sea
-1,296

Arnon (W. al Maujib)

3,346

Hebron

M O A B

Gerar

Besor

Beer-sheba

Kir-hareseth

Raphia

I D U M E A

Arabah

Zered (W. al Hasa)

31°N

Brook of Egypt (W. al 'Arish)

N e g e b

Wilderness of Zin

E D O M

Jebel Helal
2,926

34°E

36°E

Kadesh-barnea

Local grid coordinate system of 50-kilometer squares.

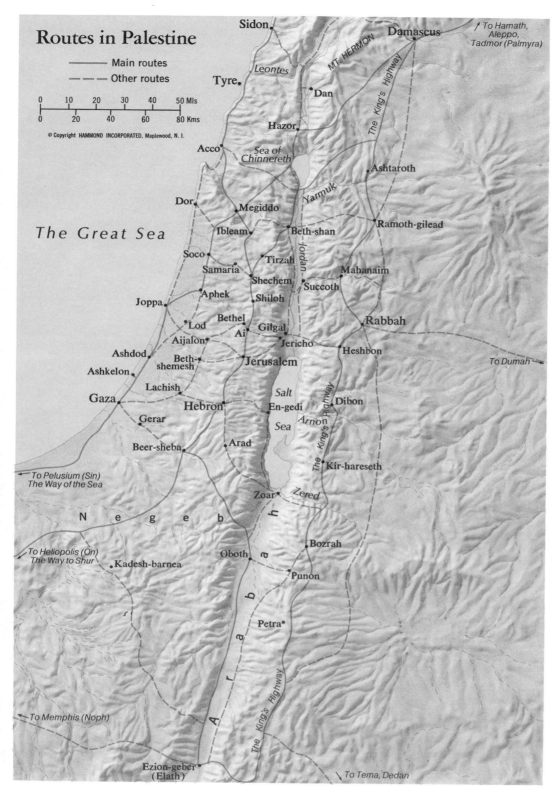

Routes in Palestine

— Main routes
--- Other routes

0 10 20 30 40 50 Mls
0 20 40 60 80 Kms
© Copyright HAMMOND INCORPORATED, Maplewood, N. J.

Sidon
Tyre
Leontes
Dan
Hazor
Acco
Sea of Chinnereth
Dor
Megiddo
Ibleam
Beth-shan
Soco
Tirzah
Samaria
Shechem
Aphek
Shiloh
Succoth
Mahanaim
Joppa
Bethel
Lod
Gilgal
Ai
Aijalon
Jericho
Ashdod
Beth-shemesh
Jerusalem
Heshbon
Ashkelon
Lachish
Salt
En-gedi
Dibon
Gaza
Hebron
Sea
Arnon
Gerar
Beer-sheba
Arad
Kir-hareseth
Zoar
Zered
Oboth
Bozrah
Kadesh-barnea
Punon
Petra
Ezion-geber (Elath)

The Great Sea
MT HERMON
Damascus
To Hamath, Aleppo, Tadmor (Palmyra)
The King's Highway
Ashtaroth
Yarmuk
Ramoth-gilead
Jordan
Rabbah
To Dumah
The King's Highway
The King's Highway
N e g e b
To Pelusium (Sin) The Way of the Sea
To Heliopolis (On) The Way to Shur
To Memphis (Noph)
A r a b a h
To Tema, Dedan

The Plain of Esdraelon looking north toward Mount Tabor.

Goats graze in the forbidding central Samaria hills, where the invading Hebrews found a home for their flocks in Biblical times.

Today children frolic in the cool waters beneath the waterfalls of En-gedi, celebrated in the Song of Songs.

The placid Dead Sea looking eastward toward the hills of Transjordan. Wind erosion at this lowest spot on earth produces an eerie, lunar landscape along the western shore.

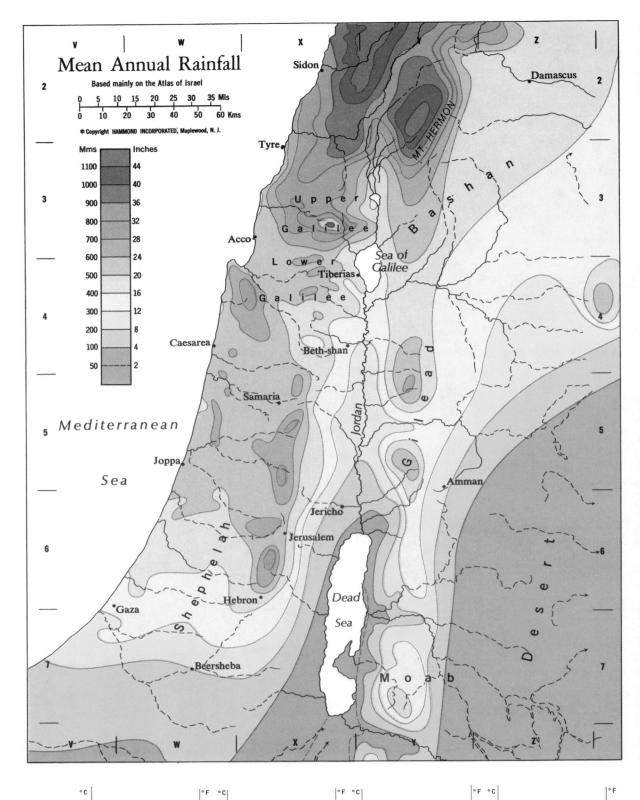

Mean Annual Rainfall

Based mainly on the Atlas of Israel

0 5 10 15 20 25 30 35 Mls
0 10 20 30 40 50 60 Kms

⊕ Copyright HAMMOND INCORPORATED, Maplewood, N. J.

Mms	Inches
1100	44
1000	40
900	36
800	32
700	28
600	24
500	20
400	16
300	12
200	8
100	4
50	2

Temperature, rainfall, and relative humidity for selected stations

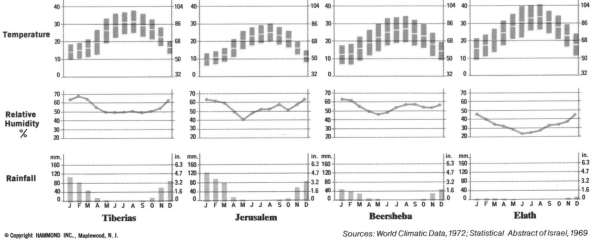

© Copyright HAMMOND INC., Maplewood, N. J.

Sources: *World Climatic Data, 1972; Statistical Abstract of Israel, 1969*

Mean Temperature January

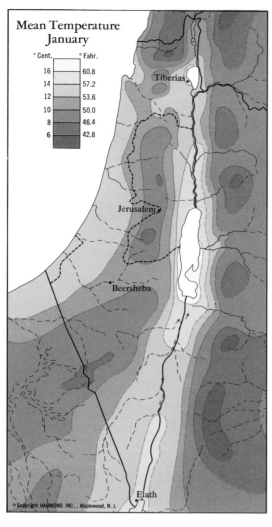

°Cent.	°Fahr.
16	60.8
14	57.2
12	53.6
10	50.0
8	46.4
6	42.8

Tiberias

Jerusalem

Beersheba

Elath

© Copyright HAMMOND INC., Maplewood, N.J.

Mean Temperature August

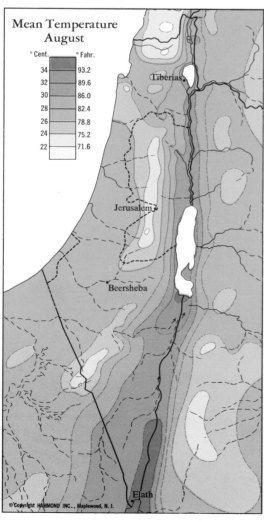

°Cent.	°Fahr.
34	93.2
32	89.6
30	86.0
28	82.4
26	78.8
24	75.2
22	71.6

Tiberias

Jerusalem

Beersheba

Elath

© Copyright HAMMOND INC., Maplewood, N.J.

Economy of Palestine

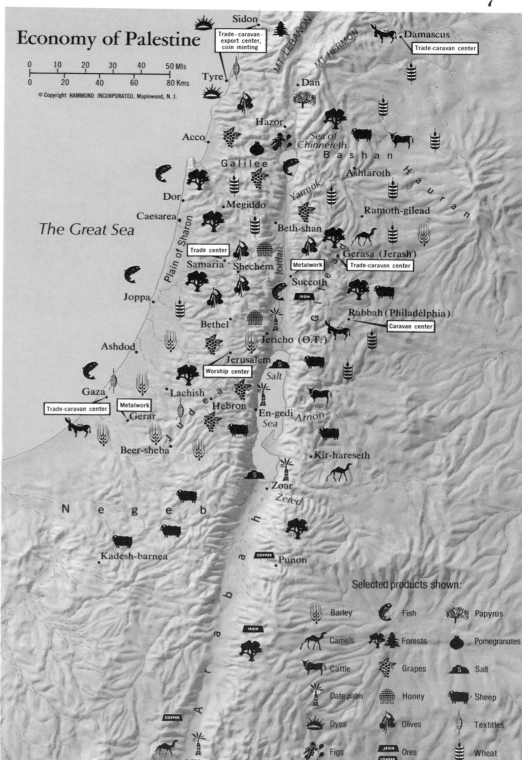

0	10	20	30	40	50 Mls
0	20	40	60	80 Kms	

© Copyright HAMMOND INCORPORATED, Maplewood, N.J.

Sidon — Trade - caravan - export center, coin minting

MT LEBANON

MT HERMON

Damascus — Trade-caravan center

Tyre

Dan

Hazor

Acco

Sea of Chinnereth

Bashan

Galilee

Ashtaroth

Dor

Ramoth-gilead

Megiddo

Caesarea

Yarmuk

Beth-shan

The Great Sea

Plain of Sharon

Trade center

Samaria

Shechem

Metalwork

Gerasa (Jerash) — Trade-caravan center

Succoth

IRON

Joppa

Jordan

Rabbah (Philadelphia) — Caravan center

Bethel

Jericho (O.T.)

Ashdod

Jerusalem — Worship center

Salt

Gaza — Trade-caravan center

Lachish

Hebron

En-gedi — Sea

Metalwork

Gerar

Arnon

Beer-sheba

Kir-hareseth

S

Zoar

Zered

N e g e b

Kadesh-barnea

COPPER — Punon

IRON

COPPER

Elath

Selected products shown:

Barley		Fish		Papyrus	
Camels		Forests		Pomegranates	
Cattle		Grapes		Salt	
Date palm		Honey		Sheep	
Dyes		Olives		Textiles	
Figs		Ores		Wheat	

Grapes being weighed in a manner reminiscent of a period when both kings and prophets in Israel were concerned with honest measure.

A cluster of dates suggests the richness and plenty of well-watered date palm plantations such as those at Jericho.

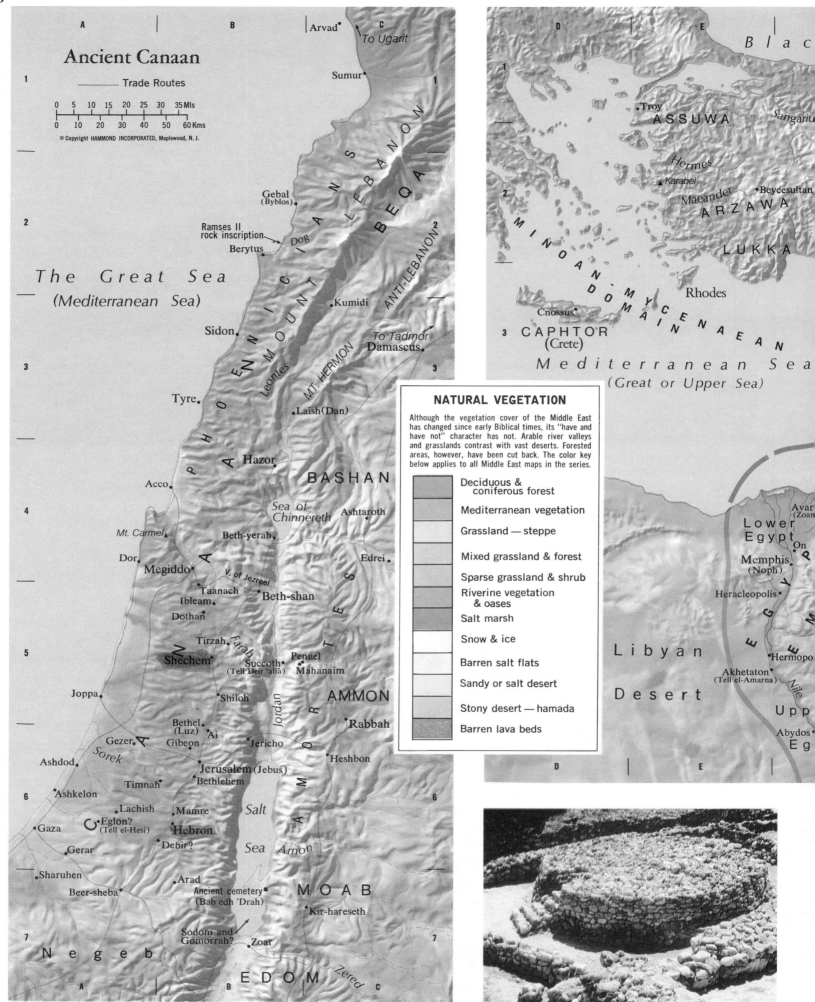

8

Ancient Canaan

—— Trade Routes

0 5 10 15 20 25 30 35 Mls
0   10   20   30   40   50   60 Kms

© Copyright HAMMOND INCORPORATED, Maplewood, N.J.

The Great Sea
(Mediterranean Sea)

Arvad
To Ugarit
Sumur

Gebal
(Byblos)

Ramses II
rock inscription →
Dog
Berytus

P H O E N I C I A N S
M O U N T
L E B A N O N
B E Q A
ANTI-LEBANON

Kumidi

Sidon

To Tadmor
Damascus

MT. HERMON

Leontes

Tyre

Laish (Dan)

Hazor

BASHAN

Acco

Ashtaroth

Sea of
Chinnereth

Mt. Carmel

Beth-yerah

Edrei

Dor

Megiddo

V. of Jezreel

Taanach
Beth-shan
Ibleam
Dothan

A   C   A   N   A   A   N

M   O   U   N   T   E   S

Tirzah
Farah
Shechem
Succoth
(Tell Deir 'allā)
Penuel
Mahanaim

Joppa

Shiloh

Jordan

AMMON

Bethel
(Luz)   Ai
Gezer   Gibeon
Sorek   Jericho   Rabbah

Ashdod
Jerusalem (Jebus)   Heshbon
Bethlehem

Ashkelon   Timnah

Lachish   Mamre   *Salt*

Gaza   Eglon?   Hebron
(Tell el-Hesi)
Debir?   *Sea*   Arnon

Gerar

Sharuhen

Arad

Beer-sheba   Ancient cemetery
(Bab edh 'Drah)   MOAB

Sodom and
Gomorrah? → Zoar   Kir-haresheth

N e g e b

E D O M

Zered

NATURAL VEGETATION

Although the vegetation cover of the Middle East has changed since early Biblical times, its "have and have not" character has not. Arable river valleys and grasslands contrast with vast deserts. Forested areas, however, have been cut back. The color key below applies to all Middle East maps in the series.

- Deciduous & coniferous forest
- Mediterranean vegetation
- Grassland — steppe
- Mixed grassland & forest
- Sparse grassland & shrub
- Riverine vegetation & oases
- Salt marsh
- Snow & ice
- Barren salt flats
- Sandy or salt desert
- Stony desert — hamada
- Barren lava beds

Blac

Troy   ASSUWA   Sangariu

Hermes

Karabel

Maeander   Beycesultan

ARZAWA

M I N O A N D

LUKKA

Rhodes

Cnossus   M Y C E N A E A N

CAPHTOR
(Crete)   D O M A I N

M e d i t e r r a n e a n   S e a
(Great or Upper Sea)

Avar
(Zoan
Lower
Egypt   On

Memphis
(Noph)

Heracleopolis

Libyan   Hermopo

Akhetaton
(Tell el-Amarna)

D e s e r t   Upp

Abydos
Eg

Nile

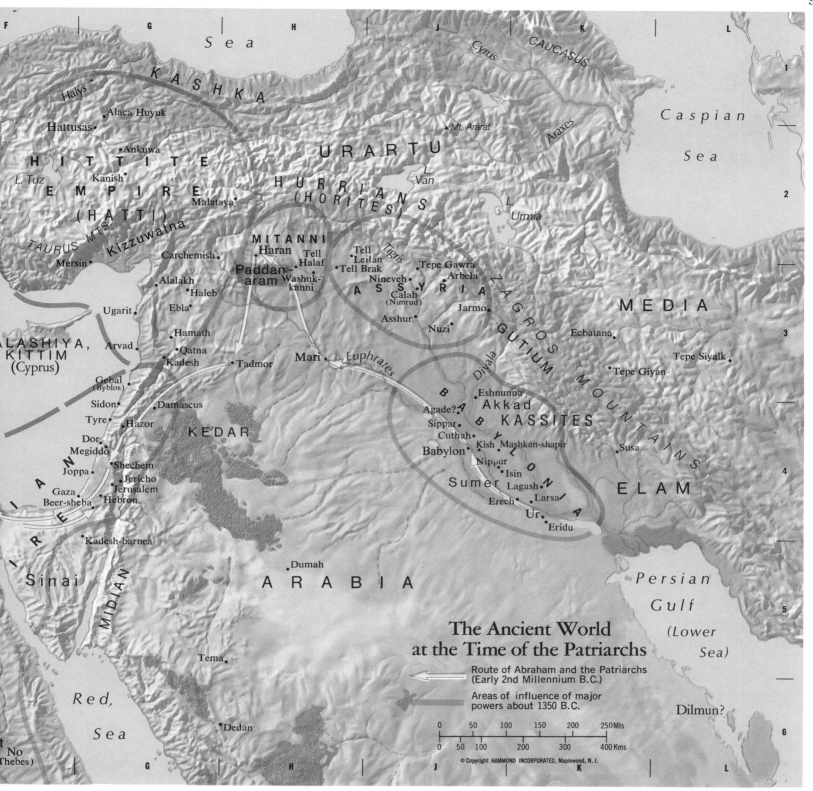

**The Ancient World
at the Time of the Patriarchs**

← Route of Abraham and the Patriarchs
(Early 2nd Millennium B.C.)

▬▬ Areas of influence of major
powers about 1350 B.C.

| 0 | 50 | 100 | 150 | 200 | 250Mls |
| 0 | 50 | 100 | 200 | 300 | 400 Kms |

© Copyright HAMMOND INCORPORATED, Maplewood, N.J.

Labels on map:
Sea · KASHKA · CAUCASUS · Caspian Sea · Cyrus · Araxes · URARTU · Mt. Ararat · Halys · Alaca Huyuk · Hattusas · Ankuwa · HITTITE EMPIRE (HATTI) · Kanish · L. Tuz · Malataya · HURRIANS (HORITES) · Van · L. Urmia · TAURUS MTS · Kizzuwatna · Mersin · MITANNI · Haran · Tell Halaf · Tell Leilan · Tell Brak · Tepe Gawra · Arbela · Tigris · MEDIA · Carchemish · Paddan-aram · Washuk-kanni · Nineveh · ASSYRIA · Calah (Nimrud) · Jarmo · ZAGROS · GUTIUM · Alalakh · Haleb · Ecbatana · Ebla · Asshur · Nuzi · Ugarit · Hamath · Tepe Siyalk · ALASHIYA, KITTIM (Cyprus) · Arvad · Qatna · Kadesh · Tadmor · Mari · Euphrates · Diyala · Tepe Giyan · MOUNTAINS · Gebal (Byblos) · Sidon · Damascus · Eshnunna · Akkad · Agade? · KASSITES · Sippar · Tyre · Hazor · KEDAR · Cuthah · Kish · Mashkan-shapir · Susa · Dor · Megiddo · Babylon · BABYLONIA · Nippur · Shechem · Joppa · Jericho · Jerusalem · Isin · ELAM · Gaza · Hebron · Sumer · Lagash · Beer-sheba · Erech · Larsa · Ur · Eridu · Kadesh-barnea · Sinai · MIDIAN · Dumah · ARABIA · Persian Gulf (Lower Sea) · Tema · No Thebes · Red Sea · Dedan · Dilmun?

In the royal tombs at Ur was found this magnificent sounding box of a lyre. The bull's head is of gold, silver and lapis lazuli. Below the head are panels of shell inlay.

The Canaanite altar for burnt offerings at Megiddo. This splendid "high place" was built in the Early Bronze Age and continued in use as late as the 19th century B.C., the time of the Hebrew Patriarchs.

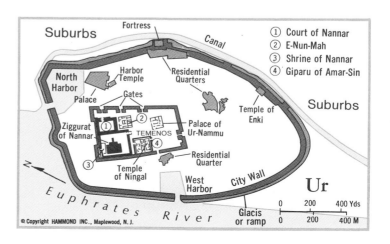

Ur

Suburbs · Fortress · Canal · Suburbs · North Harbor · Harbor Temple · Residential Quarters · Palace · Gates · Temple of Enki · Ziggurat of Nannar · TEMENOS · Palace of Ur-Nammu · Temple of Ningal · Residential Quarter · West Harbor · City Wall · Euphrates River · Glacis or ramp

① Court of Nannar
② E-Nun-Mah
③ Shrine of Nannar
④ Giparu of Amar-Sin

| 0 | 200 | 400 Yds |
| 0 | 200 | 400 M |

© Copyright HAMMOND INC., Maplewood, N.J.

10

In a timeless scene the pyramids dominate the sandy Egyptian horizon beyond the fertile fields of the Nile River plain.

A wall painting from the reign of Thutmoses III (15th century B.C.) shows the various stages of brickmaking.

The Exodus

→ Traditional route of the Exodus
⇢ Unsuccessful invasion of Canaan
— Trade routes

0 20 40 60 80Mls
0 40 80 120 Kms
© Copyright HAMMOND INCORPORATED, Maplewood, N.J.

The Great Sea
(Mediterranean Sea)

Nile Delta

Tyre
To Damascus
BASHAN
Acco · Hazor · Sea of Chinnereth · Ashtaroth
Mt. Carmel · Madon · Edrei
Dor · Megiddo
Taanach · Beth-shan
Shechem · Jabbok
Aphek · Shiloh · AMMON
Joppa · Ai · Jericho · Rabbah
Gezer · Bethel · Heshbon
Ashdod · Jerusalem · Mt. Nebo
Ashkelon · Lachish · Salt
Gaza · Eglon? · Hebron · Dibon
· Debir? · Arad · Sea · Arnon
Raphia · Beer-sheba · MOAB
· Hormah · Kir-hareseth
Negeb · Zoar · Zered
Wilderness · Ije-abarim
Jebel Maqurah · Bozrah
Lake Sirbon · Jebel Helal · Kadesh-barnea · Oboth · Punon
Pelusium (Sin)
Tanis · Baal-zephon · Zilu
The Way of the Sea · Brook of Egypt · of Zin · Sela · EDOM
Ramses · Wilderness of Shur · Jebel Harun
Goshen
Pibeseth (Bubastis) · Pithom · Succoth · The Way to Shur · Wilderness of Paran · The King's Highway
EGYPT · Bitter Lakes · Wilderness of · Mitla Pass · Ezion-geber
Heliopolis (On) · Etham · Sinai · LAND
Great Pyramids · Memphis (Noph) · Marah? · Peninsula · OF
Lake Moeris · Elim?
Crocodilopolis · Wilderness of Sin · Hazeroth? · MIDIAN
Heracleopolis · Dophkah? (Serabit el-Khadim) · Kibroth-hattaavah?
Nile · W. Feiran · Alush? Taberah?
Jebel Serbal · Rephidim?
Mt. Sinai (Jebel Musa)
(Gulf of Suez) · (Gulf of Aqaba)
Akhetaton (Tell el-Amarna) · Red Sea

Mount Tabor, where the forces of Deborah
gathered to give battle to the army of Sisera
(Judges 4:6f.). A torrent turned the Esdraelon
Plain in the foreground into a quagmire,
rendering Sisera's Canaanite chariots ineffective.

Bronze figurine of a young bull
found at a cult center on a hill
near Mt. Ebal; circa 1200 B.C.

Early Israelite Settlement in Canaan

- Area settled by Israelites
- **JUDAH** Twelve Israelite tribes
- <u>Gezer</u> Unconquered Canaanite city (according to Judges 1)

© Copyright HAMMOND INCORPORATED, Maplewood, N.J.

Sidon
Damascus 2
MT. LEBANON
HIVITES
MT. HERMON
ARAMEANS
SIDONIANS
Ahlab
Tyre
Beth-shemesh?
Dan (Laish)
DAN
Kedesh
Achzib
Merom
Beth-anath?
Hazor
Bashan
Acco
Rehob
Aphek
NAPHTALI
ZEBULUN
Sea of Chinnereth
Ashtaroth
Golan
The Great
Shimron
Mt. Tabor
Kishon
ISSACHAR
Edrei 4
Havvoth-jair
Sea
Dor
Megiddo
Jezreel
Taanach
Beth-shan
Ramoth-gilead
Dothan
Ibleam
Jabesh-gilead
Hepher
MANASSEH
Gilead
Plain of Sharon
Tirzah
Mt. Ebal
Shechem
Mt. Gerizim
Succoth
Jabbok
Jordan
AMMON 5
Aphek
Joppa
Shiloh
EPHRAIM
Bethel
Jazer
Gath
Shaalbim
Ai
Gilgal
Rabbah
Gezer
Jericho
Ekron
Sorek
DAN
Gibeon
BENJAMIN
Heshbon
Bezer
Ashdod
Aijalon
Jerusalem
Libnah
Beth-shemesh
Mt. Nebo 6
Ashkelon
Adullam
REUBEN
PHILISTINES
Gath?
Beth-zur
Salt
Gaza
Eglon?
Lachish
Hebron
Sea
Aroer
Gerar
Debir?
Arnon
Ziklag?
JUDAH
Wilderness of Judah
Arad 7
SIMEON
Beer-sheba
Hormah
MOAB
Kir-hareseth
Negeb
Zoar
Zered
Tamar
EDOM

Scale: 5 10 15 20 25 30 35 Mls / 10 20 30 40 50 60 Kms

Israel's Entry into Canaan
According to the Book of Joshua

- ⟹ Israelite campaigns
- ⟹ Canaanite campaigns

Shiloh
HIVITES
Jordan
Gath (Gittaim)
Aijalon
Ascent of Beth-horon
Bethel
Beeroth
Ai
Gilgal
Jericho
Gezer
Aijalon
Chephirah
Gibeon
Sorek
Kiriath-jearim
Ekron
JEBUSITES
Jerusalem
Qumran (City of Salt)
Makkedah
Jarmuth
Libnah
Azekah
Adullam
HITTITES
Gath?
Beth-zur
Salt
Lachish
Hebron
Sea
Eglon?
En-gedi
Debir?

Scale: 0 5 10 15 Mls / 0 5 10 15 20 25 Kms

© Copyright HAMMOND INC, Maplewood, N.J.

The fortress-temple of Baal-berith, probably
the scene of Joshua's covenant (Joshua 9:4f.),
was built at Shechem around 1650 B.C. and
with modifications continued in use throughout
the Period of the Judges.

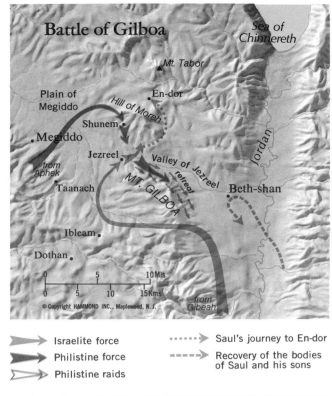

Battle of Gilboa

Sea of Chinnereth
Mt. Tabor
Plain of Megiddo
En-dor
Hill of Moreh
Shunem
Megiddo
Jezreel
from Aphek
Taanach
MT. GILBOA
Valley of Jezreel
retreat
Beth-shan
Ibleam
Jordan
Dothan
from Gibeah

0   5   10Mls
0   5   10   15Kms
© Copyright HAMMOND INC., Maplewood, N.J.

→ Israelite force
→ Philistine force
▷ Philistine raids
······▷ Saul's journey to En-dor
----▷ Recovery of the bodies of Saul and his sons

Battle of Michmash

Ophrah
Bethel
Lower Beth-horon
Upper Beth-horon
Michmash
Gilgal
Aijalon
retreat
Gibeon
Geba
to Geba
Kiriath-jearim
Gibeah
to Michmash
Jerusalem
Beth-shemesh
Bethlehem

0   5   10   15Mls
0   5   10   15   20   25Kms
© Copyright HAMMOND INC., Maplewood, N.J.

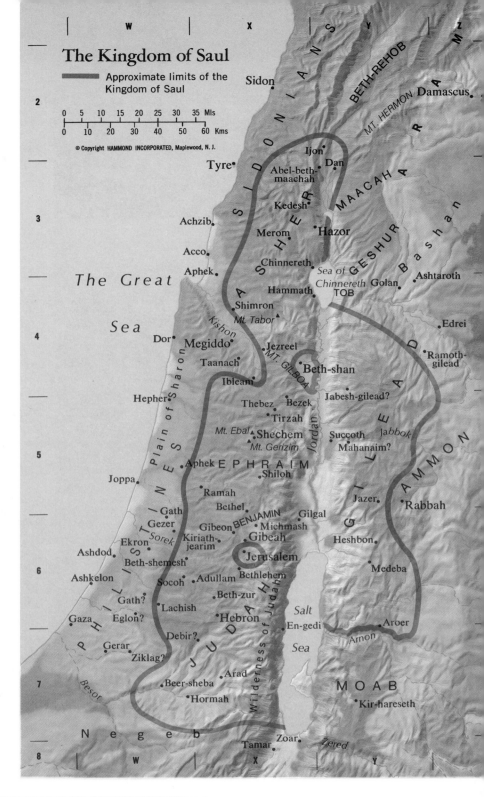

The Kingdom of Saul

━━ Approximate limits of the Kingdom of Saul

0 5 10 15 20 25 30 35 Mls
0 10 20 30 40 50 60 Kms
© Copyright HAMMOND INCORPORATED, Maplewood, N.J.

W   X   Y   Z
BETH-REHOB
Sidon
MT. HERMON   Damascus
Tyre
Ijon   Dan
Abel-beth-maachah
ASHER   MAACAH
Kedesh
Achzib
Merom   Hazor
Acco
Chinnereth   GESHUR   Bashan
Aphek
Sea of Chinnereth   Golan   Ashtaroth
Hammath   TOB
Shimron
Mt. Tabor
The Great
Kishon
Edrei
Dor   Megiddo   Jezreel   Ramoth-gilead
Sea
Taanach   MT. GILBOA   Beth-shan
Ibleam   GILEAD
Hepher
Thebez   Bezek   Jabesh-gilead?
Tirzah
Mt. Ebal   Shechem   Succoth   Jabbok
Mt. Gerizim   Mahanaim?
Aphek   EPHRAIM   Jordan   AMMON
Joppa   Shiloh
Ramah   Jazer   Rabbah
Gath   Bethel
Gezer   Gibeon   BENJAMIN   Gilgal   Heshbon
Ekron   Sorek   Kiriath-jearim   Michmash
Ashdod   Beth-shemesh   Gibeah   Medeba
Ashkelon   Socoh   Adullam   Bethlehem
Gath?   Beth-zur   Salt
Gaza   Eglon?   Lachish   Hebron   En-gedi   Aroer
Gerar   Debir?   JUDAH   Sea   Arnon
Ziklag?   Wilderness of Judah
Arad   MOAB
Beer-sheba   Kir-hareseth
Hormah
Negeb   Zoar   Zered
Tamar
PHILISTIA   Besor   Plain of Sharon   Wilderness of Judah

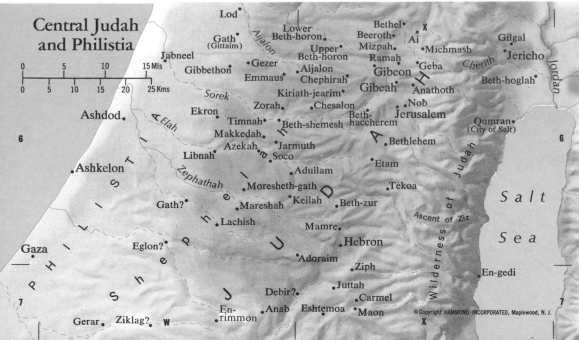

Central Judah and Philistia

0   5   10   15Mls
0   5   10   15   20   25Kms

Lod
Bethel
Lower Beth-horon   Beeroth   Ai   Gilgal
Gath (Gittaim)   Mizpah   Michmash   Jericho
Jabneel   Upper   Ramah   Geba   Cherith
Gibbethon   Beth-horon   Gibeon   Beth-hoglah
Gezer   Aijalon   Anathoth
Emmaus   Chephirah
Sorek   Kiriath-jearim   Gibeah   Jordan
Ekron   Zorah   Chesalon   Nob
Ashdod   Timnah   Beth-haccerem   Jerusalem   Qumran (City of Salt)
Elah   Beth-shemesh
Makkedah   Bethlehem
Azekah   Jarmuth   Soco   Etam   Salt
Ashkelon   Libnah   Adullam   Tekoa
Zephathah   Moresheth-gath   Beth-zur   Ascent of Ziz   Sea
Gath?   Mareshah   Keilah
Lachish   Mamre
Eglon?   Hebron   Wilderness of Judah
Gaza   Adoraim
Ziph
Gerar   Ziklag?   Debir?   Juttah   En-gedi
En-rimmon   Anab   Carmel
Eshtemoa   Maon
PHILISTIA   JUDAH

The rude remains of Saul's fortress-palace at Gibeah (background) surrounded by later construction (foreground) contrast sharply with the magnificence of Solomon's buildings.

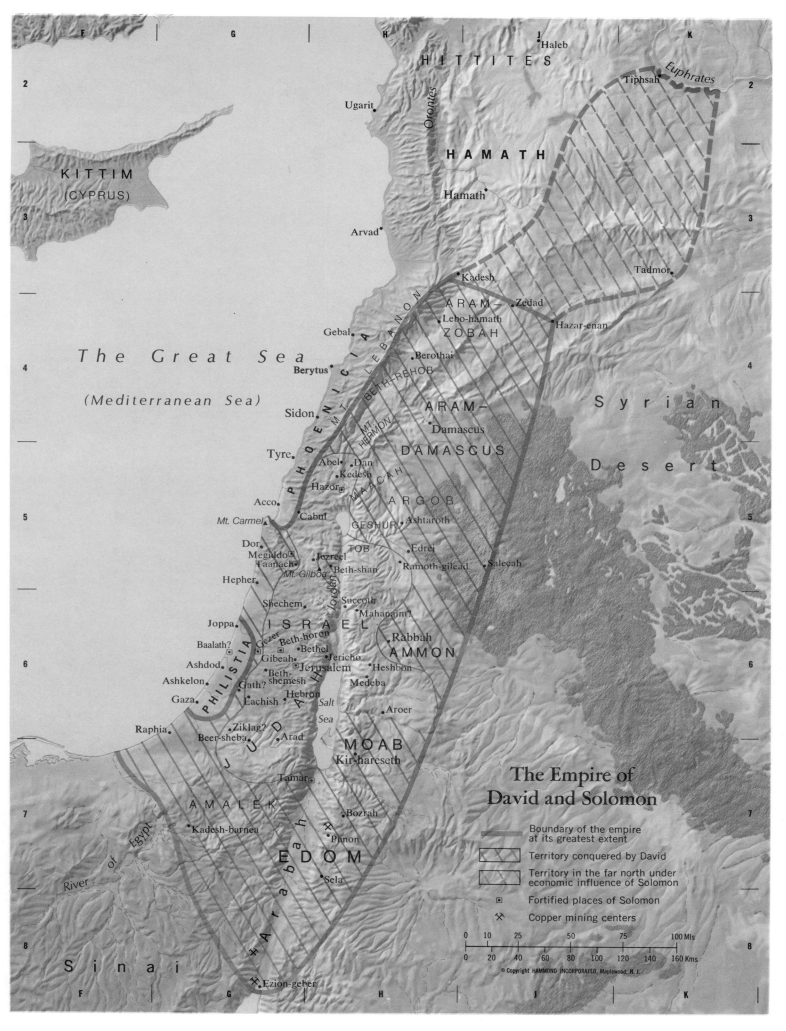

F | G | H | J | K

HITTITES

Haleb

Euphrates

2

Ugarit

Tiphsah

HAMATH

Hamath

KITTIM
(CYPRUS)

3

Arvad

Tadmor

The Great Sea

Kadesh

(Mediterranean Sea)

Zedad

ARAM —

Lebo-hamath

Hazar-enan

Gebal

ZOBAH

Berothai

Berytus

BETH-REHOB

4

ARAM —

S y r i a n

Sidon

Damascus

DAMASCUS

Tyre

Abel · Dan

D e s e r t

Kedesh

MT.
HERMON

MAACAH

Hazor

Acco

ARGOB

Cabul

Ashtaroth

5

Mt. Carmel

GESHUR

Dor

TOB

Edrei

Megiddo

Jezreel

Taanach

Beth-shan

Ramoth-gilead

Salecah

Mt. Gilboa

Hepher

Succoth

Shechem

Mahanaim?

Jordan

Joppa

ISRAEL

Rabbah

Beth-horon

AMMON

6

Baalath?

Gezer

Bethel

Gibeah

Jericho

Heshbon

Ashdod

Jerusalem

Ashkelon

Beth-
shemesh

Medeba

Gath?

Gaza

Lachish

Hebron

Salt

MOAB

Raphia

Ziklag?

Sea

Aroer

Beer-sheba

Arad

Kir-hareseth

Tamar

The Empire of
David and Solomon

AMALEK

7

Bozrah

Kadesh-barnea

Pinon

River

of

EDOM

Boundary of the empire
at its greatest extent

Egypt

Territory conquered by David

Sela

Territory in the far north under
economic influence of Solomon

□ Fortified places of Solomon

⚒ Copper mining centers

8

S i n a i

0   10   25   50   75   100 Mls

Ezion-geber

0 20 40 60 80 100 120 140 160 Kms

© Copyright HAMMOND INCORPORATED, Maplewood, N.J.

PHOENICIA   LEBANON   JUDAH   PHILISTIA   Arabah   Orontes

14

The Israelite gate at Gezer is one of the finest
Solomonic structures yet found. Its design of
two outer towers and six flanking guardrooms
is virtually identical to Solomon's fortification
gates at Megiddo and Hazor.

**Solomonic Gate
at Gezer**

0 5 10 Yds
0 5 10 M

A proto-Ionic capital of the type that
graced the gates of the royal cities and
palaces of Israel and Judah: Samaria,
Megiddo, Hazor, Ramat Rahel and
most likely Jerusalem and Gezer.

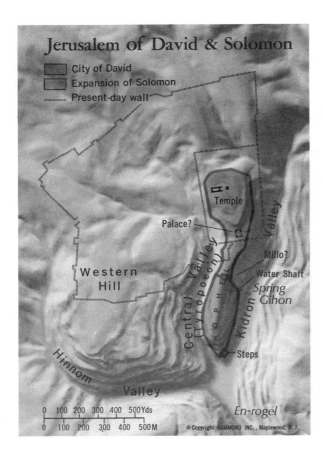

Jerusalem of David & Solomon

- City of David
- Expansion of Solomon
- Present-day wall

0 100 200 300 400 500Yds
0 100 200 300 400 500M

© Copyright HAMMOND INC., Maplewood, N.J.

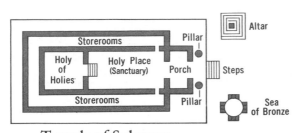

Temple of Solomon

Storerooms	Pillar
Holy of Holies	Holy Place (Sanctuary)	Porch
Storerooms	Pillar

Altar · Steps · Sea of Bronze

0 10 20 30 Cubits
0 5 10 15 M

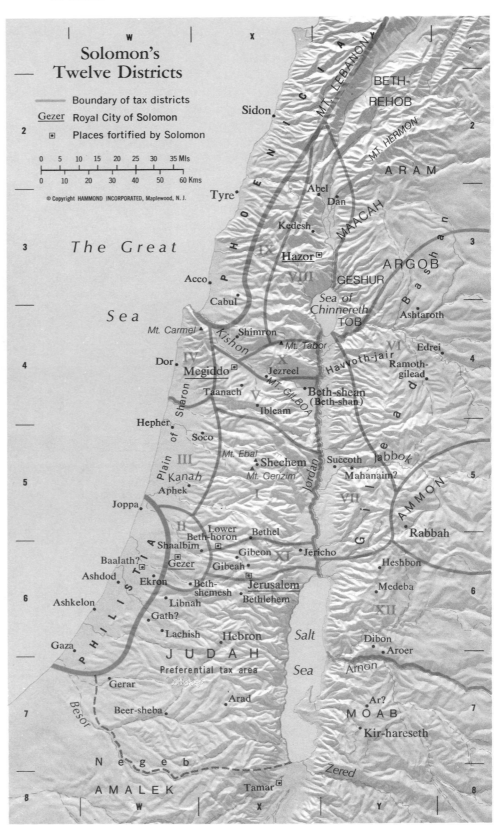

Solomon's Twelve Districts

Boundary of tax districts
Gezer Royal City of Solomon
▫ Places fortified by Solomon

0 5 10 15 20 25 30 35 Mls
0 10 20 30 40 50 60 Kms

© Copyright HAMMOND INCORPORATED, Maplewood, N.J.

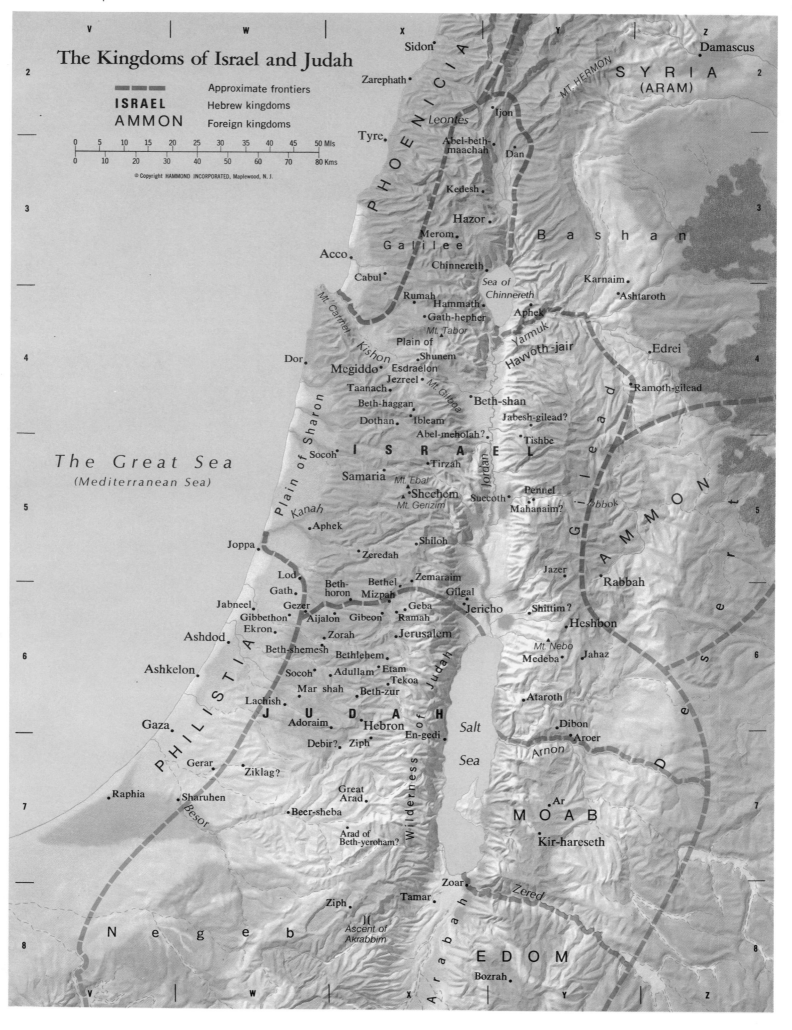

The Kingdoms of Israel and Judah

ISRAEL — — — Approximate frontiers
AMMON   Hebrew kingdoms
               Foreign kingdoms

0 5 10 15 20 25 30 35 40 45 50 Mls
0 10 20 30 40 50 60 70 80 Kms

© Copyright HAMMOND INCORPORATED, Maplewood, N. J.

PHOENICIA
SYRIA (ARAM)
Damascus

Sidon
Zarephath
Tyre
Leontes
Ijon
Abel-beth-maachah
Dan
Kedesh
Hazor
Merom
Galilee
Acco
Chinnereth
Cabul
Karnaim
Ashtaroth
Rumah
Sea of Chinnereth
Hammath
Gath-hepher
Aphek
Mt. Tabor
Yarmuk
Hawvoth-jair
Edrei
Plain of Esdraelon
Shunem
Ramoth-gilead
Dor
Mt. Gilboa
Megiddo
Jezreel
Beth-shan
Taanach
Jabesh-gilead?
Beth-haggan
ISRAEL
Tishbe
Dothan
Ibleam
Abel-meholah?
Socoh
Tirzah
Jordan
Gilead

The Great Sea
(Mediterranean Sea)

Samaria
Mt. Ebal
Shechem
Mt. Gerizim
Succoth
Pennel
Mahanaim?
Jabbok
AMMON
Plain of Sharon
Kanah
Aphek
Joppa
Shiloh
Zeredah
Jazer
Rabbah
Lod
Zemaraim
Gath
Beth-horon
Bethel
Mizpah
Gilgal
Heshbon
Jabneel
Gezer
Geba
Jericho
Shittim?
Gibbethon
Aijalon
Gibeon
Ramah
Ekron
Zorah
Jerusalem
Ashdod
Mt. Nebo
Medeba
Beth-shemesh
Bethlehem
Jahaz
Ashkelon
Socoh
Adullam
Etam
Mar shah
Tekoa
Beth-zur
Lachish
JUDAH
Ataroth
Gaza
Adoraim
Hebron
En-gedi
Salt Sea
Dibon
Aroer
Debir?
Ziph
Arnon
Gerar
Wilderness of Judah
Ar
Ziklag?
MOAB
Raphia
Sharuhen
Great Arad
Kir-hareseth
Beer-sheba
Besor
Arad of Beth-yeroham?
Zoar
Zered
Ziph
Tamar
Negeb
Ascent of Akrabbim
Arabah
EDOM
Bozrah

PHILISTIA
Mt. Carmel
Kishon

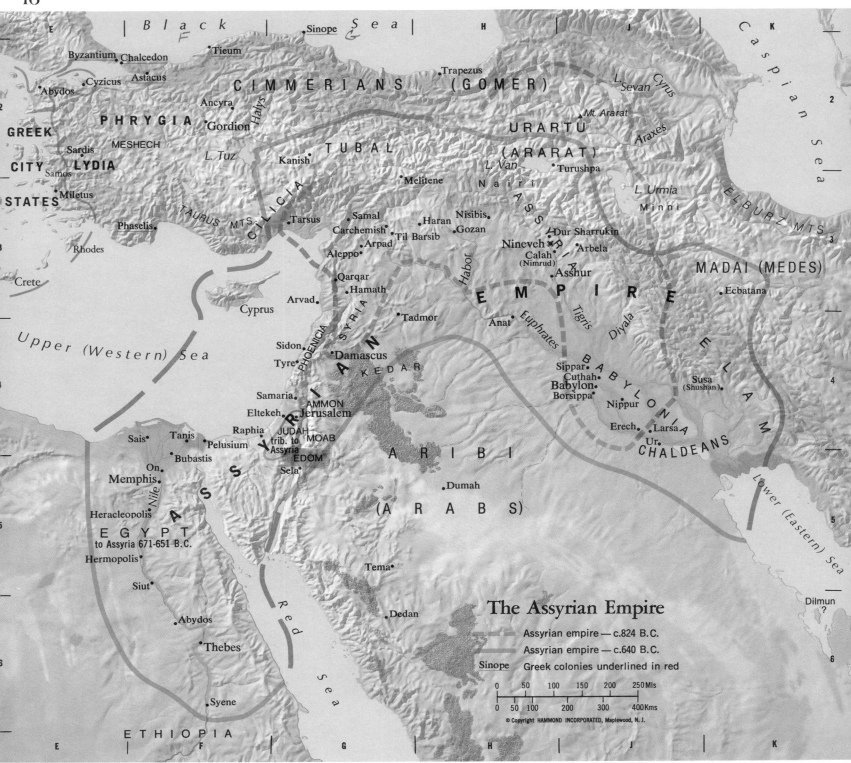

The Assyrian Empire

--- Assyrian empire — c.824 B.C.
--- Assyrian empire — c.640 B.C.

Sinope   Greek colonies underlined in red

0   50   100   150   200   250 Mls
0   50   100   200   300   400 Kms

© Copyright HAMMOND INCORPORATED, Maplewood, N.J.

Tiglath-pileser III extended the Assyrian Empire in the 8th century B.C. and caused political chaos in Israel.

The only contemporary picture of a Hebrew monarch occurs on the Black Obelisk, an Assyrian monument from Nimrud. It shows Jehu, on his knees before Shalmaneser III.

Assyrian wall relief from the throne room of Sennacherib shows Hebrews fleeing the doomed city of Lachish in southwest Judah when it was under Assyrian siege in 701 B.C.

Nineveh

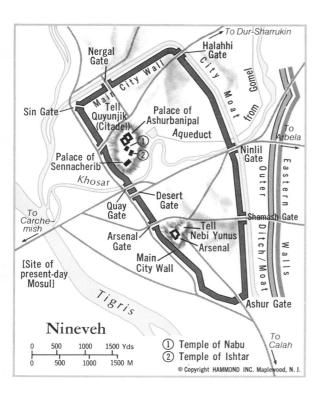

Nergal Gate
Halahhi Gate
To Dur-Sharrukin
To Arbela
Main City Wall
City Wall
City Moat from Gomel
Sin Gate
Tell Quyunjik (Citadel)
Palace of Ashurbanipal
Aqueduct
Ninlil Gate
Palace of Sennacherib
Khosar
Desert Gate
To Carche-mish
Quay Gate
Outer Ditch/Moat
Eastern Walls
Shamash Gate
Arsenal Gate
Tell Nebi Yunus
Arsenal
Main City Wall
[Site of present-day Mosul]
Tigris
Ashur Gate
To Calah

① Temple of Nabu
② Temple of Ishtar

0 500 1000 1500 Yds
0 500 1000 1500 M
© Copyright HAMMOND INC. Maplewood, N.J.

Babylon

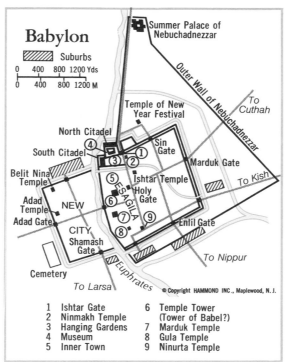

Summer Palace of Nebuchadnezzar
Suburbs
0 400 800 1200 Yds
0 400 1200 M
Temple of New Year Festival
Outer Wall of Nebuchadnezzar
To Cuthah
North Citadel
South Citadel
Sin Gate
Marduk Gate
Belit Nina Temple
Ishtar Temple
ESAGILA
Holy Gate
To Kish
Adad Temple
NEW
Adad Gate
CITY
Shamash Gate
Enlil Gate
To Nippur
Cemetery
Euphrates
To Larsa
© Copyright HAMMOND INC., Maplewood, N.J.

1 Ishtar Gate
2 Ninmakh Temple
3 Hanging Gardens
4 Museum
5 Inner Town
6 Temple Tower (Tower of Babel?)
7 Marduk Temple
8 Gula Temple
9 Ninurta Temple

A reconstruction of the Ishtar Gate at Babylon, with the famous "hanging gardens" in the right background. The king entering the gate is Nebuchadnezzar II (605-562 B.C.), who destroyed Jerusalem.

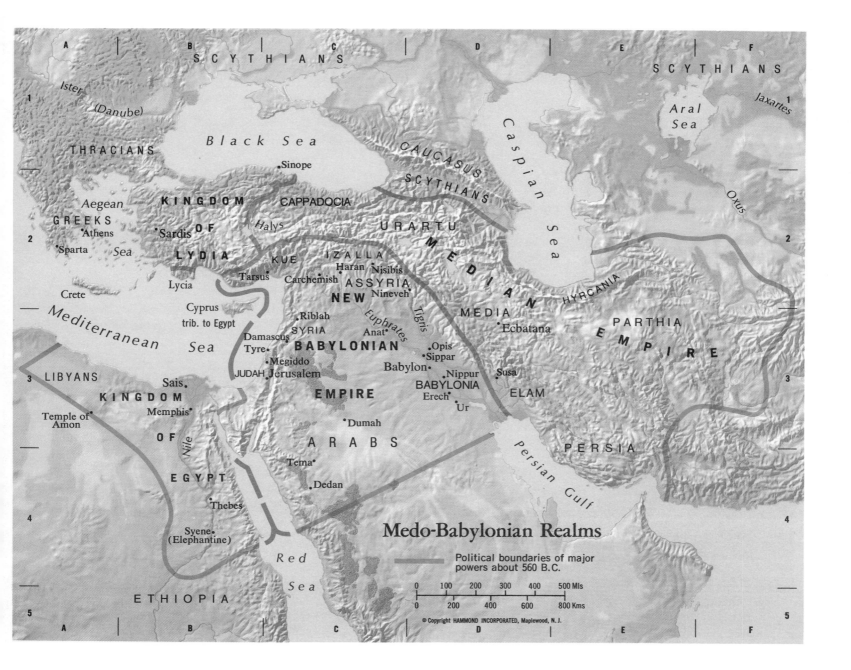

Medo-Babylonian Realms

Political boundaries of major powers about 560 B.C.

0 100 200 300 400 500 Mls
0 200 400 600 800 Kms
© Copyright HAMMOND INCORPORATED, Maplewood, N.J.

18

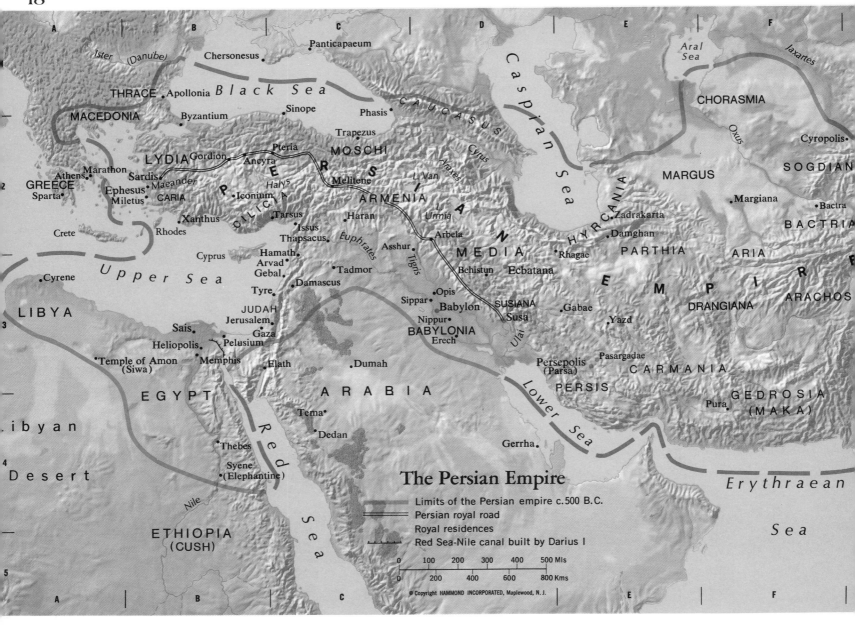

The Persian Empire

Limits of the Persian empire c.500 B.C.
Persian royal road
Royal residences
Red Sea-Nile canal built by Darius I

| 0 | 100 | 200 | 300 | 400 | 500 Mls |
| 0 | 200 | 400 | 600 | 800 Kms |

© Copyright HAMMOND INCORPORATED, Maplewood, N.J.

On this clay cylinder of 538 B.C., Cyrus provides royal authorization for the rebuilding of temples "beyond the Euphrates."

Tomb of Cyrus the Great at Pasargadae, Iran. When he conquered Babylon, Cyrus allowed the Jews to return to Jerusalem and rebuild their temple.

The earliest coin used in the Holy Land is this 4th-century silver Persian piece. The obverse has a falcon with the inscription "Yahud." The reverse has a lily with no inscription.

Jerusalem After the Exile

Post-exilic city
Expansion of city
Present-day wall

Large-scale expansion of the city to the west began again under Nehemiah at the remains of the "Broad Wall" found west of the Temple Mount.

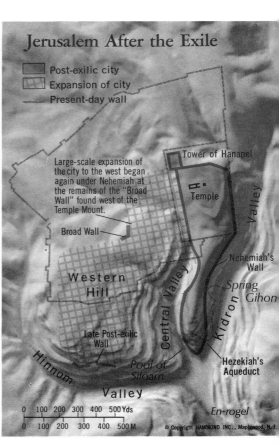

| 0 | 100 | 200 | 300 | 400 | 500 Yds |
| 0 | 100 | 200 | 300 | 400 | 500 M |

© Copyright HAMMOND INC., Maplewood, N.J.

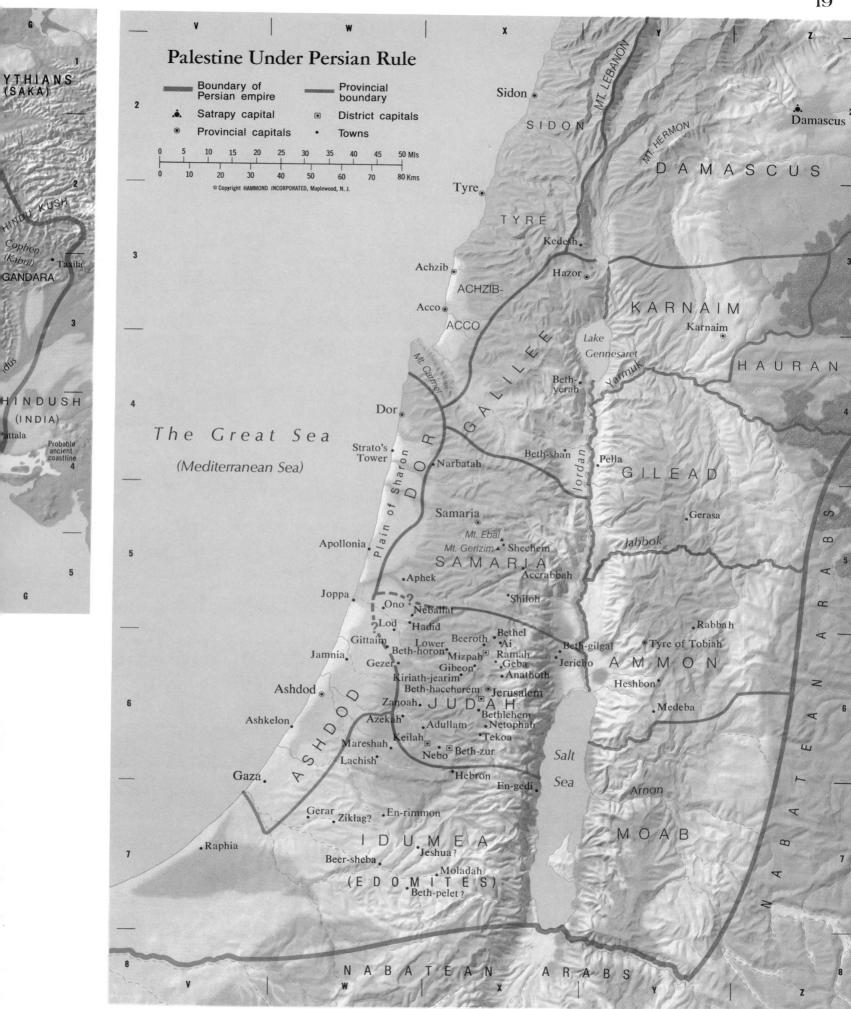

Palestine Under Persian Rule

Boundary of Persian empire — **Provincial boundary**

⚊ Satrapy capital — ☐ District capitals

◉ Provincial capitals — • Towns

Scale:
0 5 10 15 20 25 30 35 40 45 50 Mis
0 10 20 30 40 50 60 70 80 Kms

© Copyright HAMMOND INCORPORATED, Maplewood, N.J.

YTHIANS
(SAKA)

HINDU KUSH

Cophen
(Kabul)

GANDARA

• Taxila

HINDUSH

(INDIA)

attala

Probable
ancient
coastline

The Great Sea

(Mediterranean Sea)

Sidon

SIDON

MT. LEBANON

MT. HERMON

Damascus

D A M A S C U S

Tyre

TYRE

Kedesh •

Achzib ◉

ACHZIB-

Hazor ◉

K A R N A I M

Acco ◉

ACCO

Karnaim ◉

H A U R A N

Mt. Carmel

*Lake
Gennesaret*

Beth-
yerah

Yarmuk

Dor ◉

Strato's
Tower

• Narbatah

Beth-shan

Pella •

Jordan

G I L E A D

Samaria

Mt. Ebal

Mt. Gerizim ▲ • Shechem

Jabbok

Gerasa •

Apollonia

Plain of Sharon

S A M A R I A

Accrabbah •

Joppa

• Aphek

• Shiloh

Ono

? Neballat

Lod

Hadid

Gittaim

Lower

Beeroth

Bethel

• Ai

Beth-gilgal

• Tyre of Tobiah

Jamnia

Beth-horon

Mizpah ☐

Ramah

Geba

Jericho

A M M O N

Gezer

Gibeon •

• Anathoth

Heshbon •

Kiriath-jearim

Beth-haccherem

☐ Jerusalem

Ashdod ◉

Zanoah

J U D A H

Bethlehem

Medeba •

Ashkelon

Azekah

Adullam

Netophah

Keilah

• Tekoa

Mareshah

Nebo

Beth-zur

Salt

Lachish

Sea

Gaza

• Hebron

En-gedi •

Arnon

Gerar

Ziklag?

• En-rimmon

M O A B

• Raphia

I D U M E A

Jeshua?

Beer-sheba

Moladah

(E D O M I T E S)

Beth-pelet ?

N A B A T E A N   A R A B S

N A B A T E A N   A R A B S

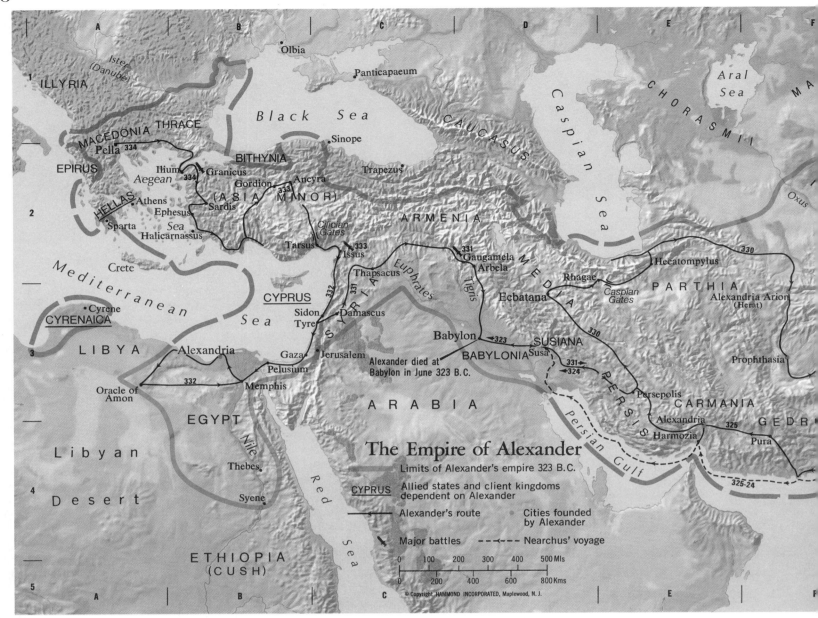

Black Sea

Olbia

Panticapaeum

ILLYRIA

Ister (Danube)

MACEDONIA THRACE

Pella 334

EPIRUS

Aegean

HELLAS

Athens

Sparta

Crete

Ilium

Granicus 334

Gordion

Ancyra 333

BITHYNIA

Sinope

Trapezus

CAUCASUS

ARMENIA

(ASIA MINOR)

Sardis

Ephesus

Sea

Halicarnassus

Mediterranean

Sea

Cyrene

CYRENAICA

LIBYA

Alexandria

Oracle of Amon 332

Memphis

Gaza

Pelusium

Jerusalem

Libyan

Desert

Thebes

Syene

EGYPT

Red Sea

ETHIOPIA (CUSH)

CYPRUS

Cilician Gates

Tarsus

Issus 333

Thapsacus

Sidon

Tyre

Damascus

SYRIA

Euphrates

Gaugamela 331

Arbela

Tigris

Ecbatana

MEDIA

Babylon 323

BABYLONIA

Susa

SUSIANA 331 324

ARABIA

Caspian Sea

Rhagae

Caspian Gates

Hecatompylus 330

PARTHIA

Alexandria Arion (Herat)

Prophthasia

PERSIS

Persepolis

Persian Gulf

Harmozia

Alexandria 325

Pura

CARMANIA

GEDR

325-24

Aral Sea

CHORASMII

Oxus

The Empire of Alexander

Limits of Alexander's empire 323 B.C.

CYPRUS — Allied states and client kingdoms dependent on Alexander

Alexander's route

Major battles

Cities founded by Alexander

Nearchus' voyage

Alexander died at Babylon in June 323 B.C.

0 100 200 300 400 500 Mls
0 200 400 600 800 Kms

© Copyright HAMMOND INCORPORATED, Maplewood, N.J.

Alexander the Great at the Battle of Issus, where he defeated the Persians. This Roman mosaic from Pompeii shows the determination of this brilliant soldier who established an empire at age thirty.

Silver tetradrachm of Ptolemy I struck in Egypt shows Alexander wearing an elephant head-dress. Reverse: the goddess Athena.

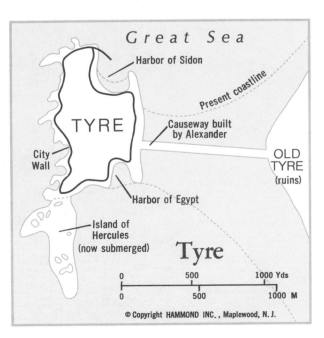

Great Sea

Harbor of Sidon

Present coastline

TYRE

Causeway built by Alexander

OLD TYRE (ruins)

City Wall

Harbor of Egypt

Island of Hercules (now submerged)

Tyre

0 500 1000 Yds
0 500 1000 M

© Copyright HAMMOND INC., Maplewood, N.J.

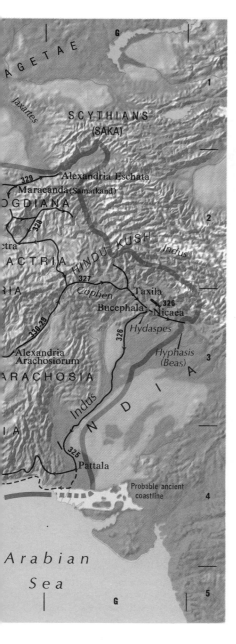

Massive round towers such as this one were set into Israelite walls at Samaria by Alexander's military engineers. Samaria, once capital of Israel, became one of the most Hellenized cities of Palestine.

Seleucus I, "Nicator," continued Alexander's Hellenizing policies.

Ptolemy I, "Soter," turned Egypt into his personal domain.

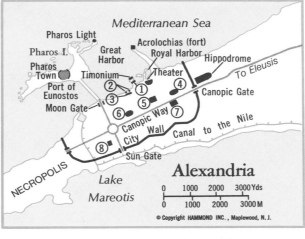

Alexandria

1 Poseidium
2 Obelisks (later Cleopatra's Needles)
3 Caesarium
4 Stadium
5 Library and Museum
6 Amphitheater
7 Sports Grounds
8 Serapeion

Terracotta statuette of a war elephant with driver and tower.

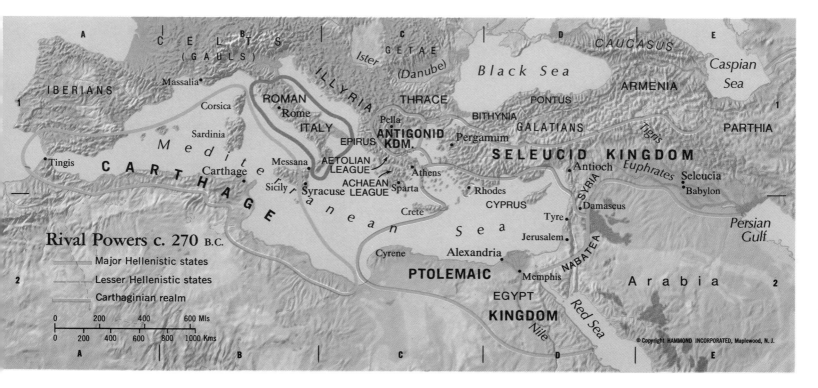

Rival Powers c. 270 B.C.

— Major Hellenistic states
— Lesser Hellenistic states
— Carthaginian realm

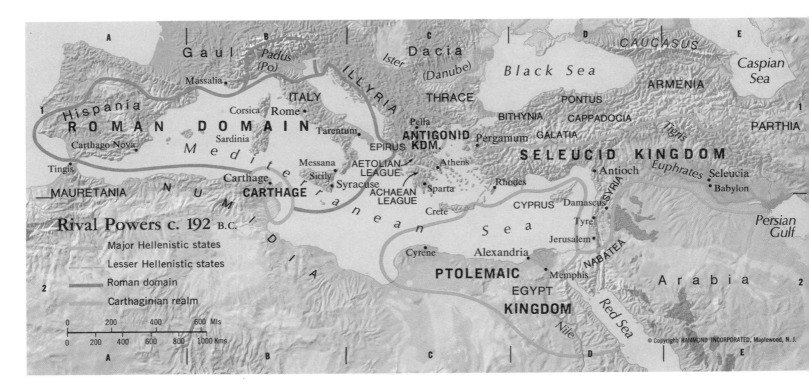

Antiochus III, "The Great," who took Palestine from the Ptolemies at the Battle of Panias in 197 B.C.

Naked Greek youths participating in athletic contests are pictured on this 6th-century B.C. Greek vase. Such practices introduced into Jerusalem were a cause of the Maccabean Revolt.

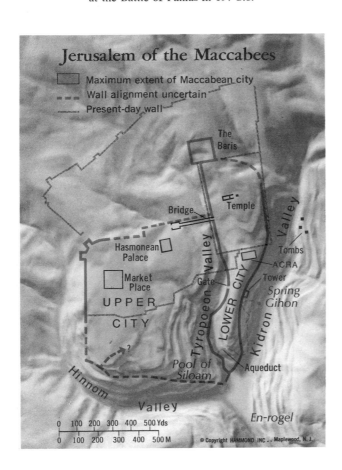

Jerusalem of the Maccabees

- Maximum extent of Maccabean city
- Wall alignment uncertain
- Present-day wall

Antiochus IV, "Epiphanes," tried to Hellenize the Jews, which led to the Maccabean War in 166 B.C.

A lepton of Alexander Jannaeus (103-76 B.C.), who expanded the Jewish Hasmonean Kingdom to its greatest limits. This coin is popularly known as the "widow's mite" of the New Testament.

A Jewish "slipper lamp" from the time of the Hasmonean Kingdom.

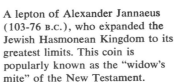

Antigonus II (40-37 B.C.), the last of the Hasmonean rulers, issued debased coinage, but did show the Menorah on some coins such as this perutah. He lost his throne to Herod the Great.

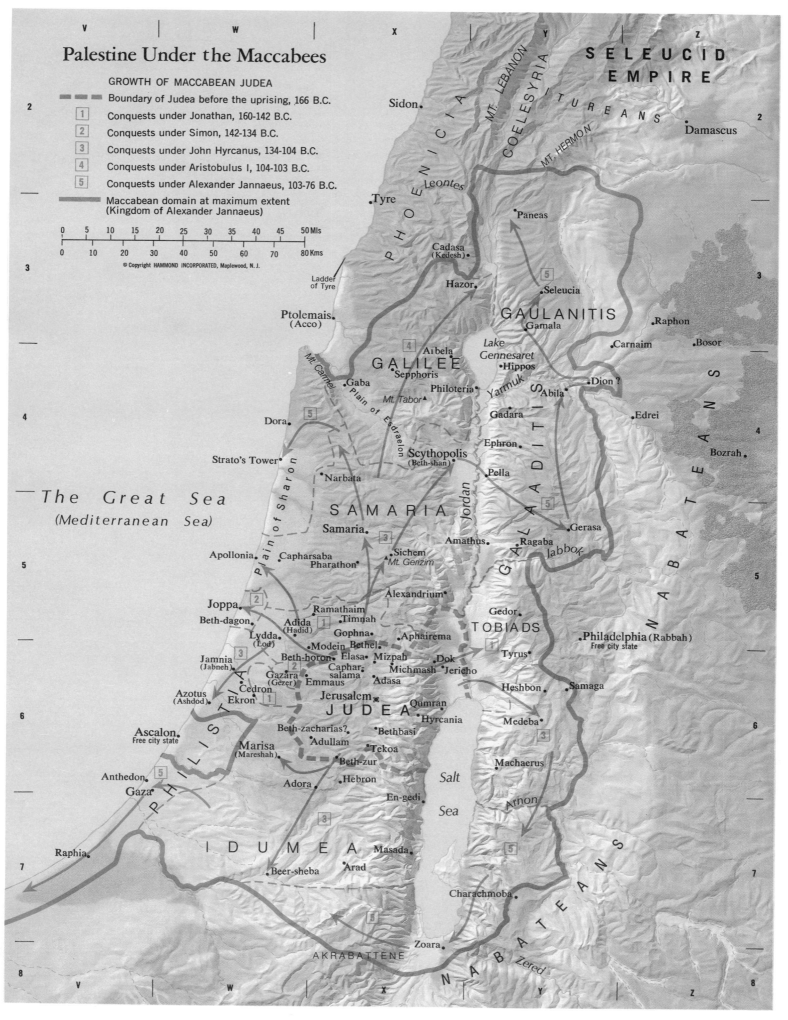

Palestine Under the Maccabees

GROWTH OF MACCABEAN JUDEA

- – – Boundary of Judea before the uprising, 166 B.C.
- [1] Conquests under Jonathan, 160-142 B.C.
- [2] Conquests under Simon, 142-134 B.C.
- [3] Conquests under John Hyrcanus, 134-104 B.C.
- [4] Conquests under Aristobulus I, 104-103 B.C.
- [5] Conquests under Alexander Jannaeus, 103-76 B.C.
- —— Maccabean domain at maximum extent (Kingdom of Alexander Jannaeus)

© Copyright HAMMOND INCORPORATED, Maplewood, N.J.

SELEUCID EMPIRE

PHOENICIA · COELESYRIA · ITUREANS

Sidon · Damascus · Tyre · Paneas · Cadasa (Kedesh) · Seleucia

GAULANITIS · Gamala · Raphon · Carnaim · Bosor

Hazor · Ptolemais (Acco)

GALILEE · Arbela · Sepphoris · Lake Gennesaret · Hippos · Dion? · Edrei · Bozrah

Gaba · Philoteria · Abila · Gadara · Ephron · Pella

Dora · Strato's Tower · Scythopolis (Beth-shan)

The Great Sea (Mediterranean Sea)

Narbata · SAMARIA · Samaria · Amathus · Ragaba · Gerasa

Apollonia · Capharsaba · Pharathon · Sichem · Mt. Gerizim

Alexandrium · TOBIADS · Gedor · Philadelphia (Rabbah)

Joppa · Ramathaim · Timnah · Gophna · Aphairema · Tyrus

Beth-dagon · Adida (Hadid) · Bethel · Heshbon · Samaga

Lydda (Lod) · Modein · Elasa · Mizpah · Dok · Michmash · Jericho

Jamnia (Jabneh) · Beth-horon · Caphar-salama · Adasa · Medeba

Gazara (Gezer) · Emmaus · Jerusalem · Qumran · Hyrcania

Azotus (Ashdod) · Cedron · Ekron · JUDEA · Bethbasi

Ascalon · Beth-zacharias? · Adullam · Tekoa · Machaerus

Marisa (Mareshah) · Beth-zur · En-gedi · Salt Sea

Anthedon · Adora · Hebron · Arnon

Gaza · PHILISTIA · IDUMEA · Masada · Arad

Raphia · Beer-sheba · Charachmoba

AKRABATTENE · Zoara · NABATEANS · Zered

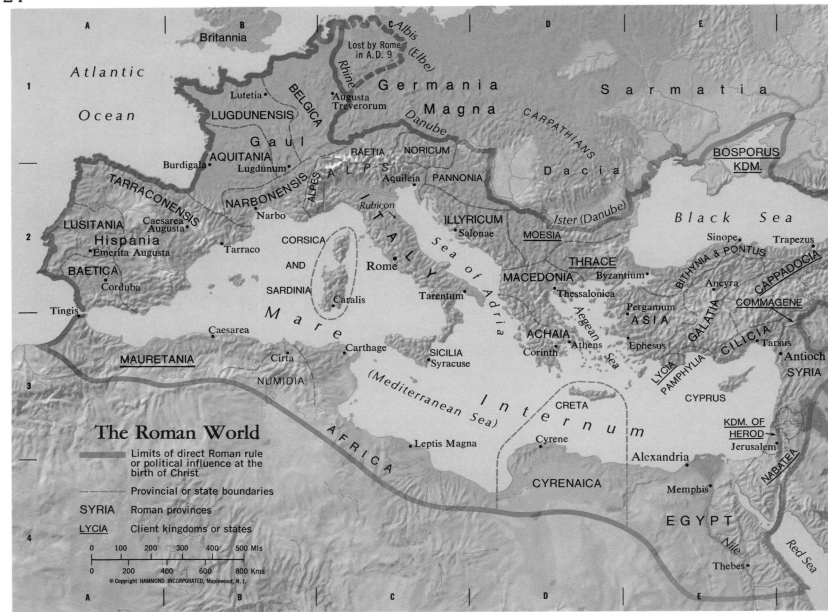

The Roman World

Limits of direct Roman rule or political influence at the birth of Christ

Provincial or state boundaries

SYRIA   Roman provinces

LYCIA   Client kingdoms or states

| 0 | 100 | 200 | 300 | 400 | 500 Mls |
| 0 | 200 | 400 | 600 | 800 Kms |

© Copyright HAMMOND INCORPORATED, Maplewood, N.J.

Senate House in the Imperial Forum.

Octavian (Caesar-Augustus).

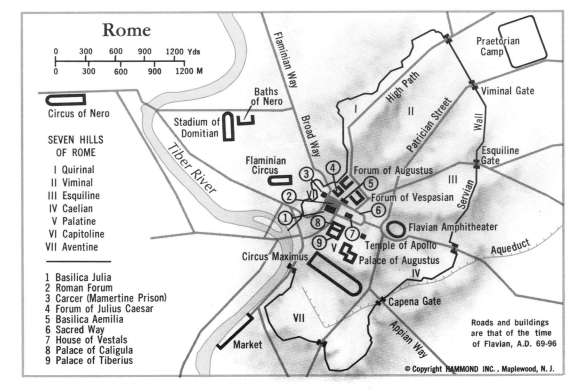

Rome

| 0 | 300 | 600 | 900 | 1200 Yds |
| 0 | 300 | 600 | 900 | 1200 M |

Circus of Nero

SEVEN HILLS
OF ROME

I   Quirinal
II   Viminal
III Esquiline
IV   Caelian
V   Palatine
VI   Capitoline
VII Aventine

1 Basilica Julia
2 Roman Forum
3 Carcer (Mamertine Prison)
4 Forum of Julius Caesar
5 Basilica Aemilia
6 Sacred Way
7 House of Vestals
8 Palace of Caligula
9 Palace of Tiberius

Roads and buildings are that of the time of Flavian, A.D. 69-96

© Copyright HAMMOND INC., Maplewood, N.J.

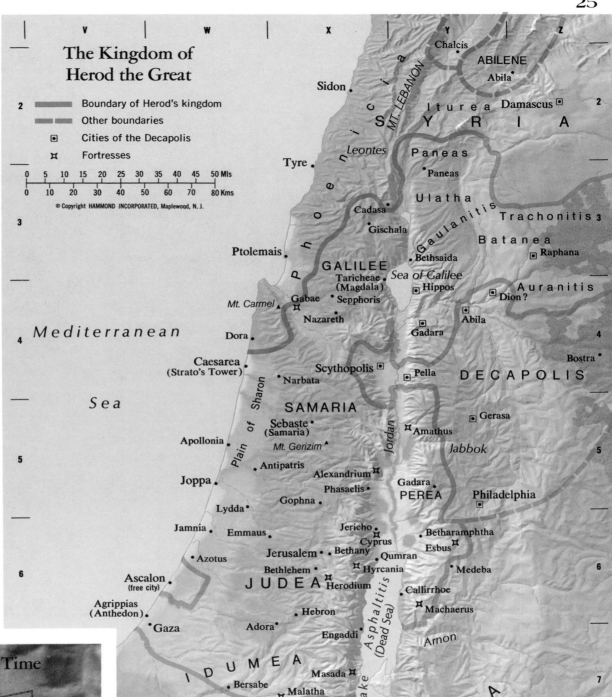

The Kingdom of Herod the Great

	Boundary of Herod's kingdom
	Other boundaries
⊡	Cities of the Decapolis
⋈	Fortresses

0 5 10 15 20 25 30 35 40 45 50 Mls
0 10 20 30 40 50 60 70 80 Kms

© Copyright HAMMOND INCORPORATED, Maplewood, N.J.

Map labels:

Rha (Volga)
Caspian Sea
CAUCASUS
Colchis Iberia Albania
ARMENIA
Artaxata
PARTHIAN EMPIRE
Tigris Euphrates Ctesiphon
Arabia

Chalcis
ABILENE
Abila
Sidon
SYRIA
Iturea Damascus ⊡
MT. LEBANON
Leontes Paneas
Tyre Paneas
Ulatha
Cadasa Gaulanitis Trachonitis
Gischala Batanea
Ptolemais Bethsaida Raphana ⊡
GALILEE Auranitis
Taricheae (Magdala) Sea of Galilee
Mt. Carmel Gabae ⋈ Sepphoris Hippos ⊡ Dion ? ⊡
Nazareth Abila ⊡
Dora Gadara ⊡
Mediterranean Sea
Caesarea (Strato's Tower) Scythopolis ⊡ Pella ⊡ DECAPOLIS Bostra
Narbata
Plain of Sharon SAMARIA
Sebaste (Samaria) Gerasa ⊡
Apollonia Mt. Gerizim Amathus ⋈ Jabbok
Antipatris
Joppa Alexandrium ⋈ Gadara ⋈ Philadelphia ⊡
Phasaelis PEREA
Lydda Gophna
Jamnia Emmaus Jericho Betharamphtha
Cyprus Esbus ⋈
Azotus Jerusalem Bethany Qumran
Bethlehem Hyrcania ⋈ Medeba
Ascalon (free city) JUDEA Herodium ⋈ Callirrhoe
Agrippias (Anthedon) Adora Machaerus ⋈
Gaza Hebron Engaddi Arnon
IDUMEA Lake Asphaltitis (Dead Sea)
Masada ⋈
Bersabe Malatha ⋈
Elusa NABATEA
Khirbet Tannur Nabatean sanctuary
Nessana
Jordan

Jerusalem in Herod's Time

- ——— Ancient city walls
- – – – Wall alignment uncertain
- ········ Present-day wall

Pool of Bethzatha (Bethesda)
Fortress Antonia
WALL
SECOND QUARTER
Golden Gate
Tunnel
THE TEMPLE
Solomon's Porch
FIRST WALL Bridge
Royal Portico
Towers & Palace of Herod Staircase
Market Place Huldah Gates
UPPER CITY
Theater? Hippodrome?
LOWER CITY
Spring Gihon
Kidron Valley
Tyropoeon Valley
Hinnom Valley
FIRST WALL
Pool of Siloam

0 100 200 300 400 500 Yds
0 100 200 300 400 500 M

© Copyright HAMMOND INC., Maplewood, N.J.

Temple of Herod

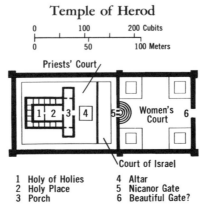

0 100 200 Cubits
0 50 100 Meters

Priests' Court
Women's Court
Court of Israel

1 Holy of Holies
2 Holy Place
3 Porch
4 Altar
5 Nicanor Gate
6 Beautiful Gate?

Model of Herod's Temple, with surrounding courts and Royal Portico in the background.

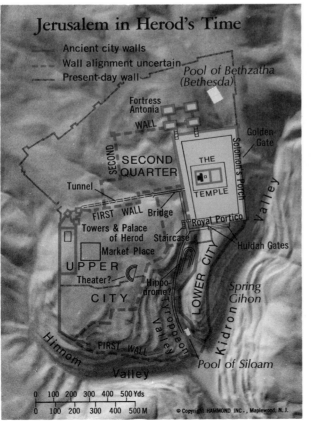

26

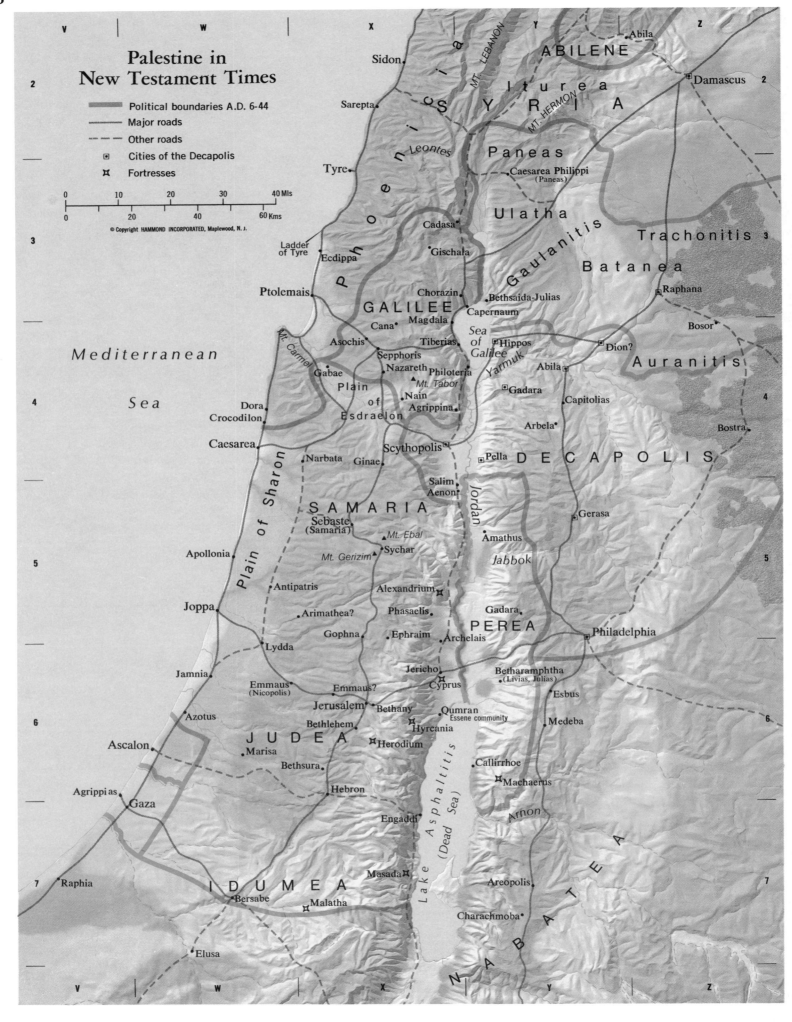

Palestine in New Testament Times

Political boundaries A.D. 6-44
Major roads
Other roads
⊡ Cities of the Decapolis
⋈ Fortresses

0   10   20   30   40 Mls
0   20   40   60 Kms

© Copyright HAMMOND INCORPORATED, Maplewood, N.J.

Abila
ABILENE
Sidon
Iturea
SYRIA
MT. LEBANON
Damascus
Sarepta
MT. HERMON
Paneas
Tyre
Leontes
Caesarea Philippi
(Paneas)
Ulatha
Trachonitis
Ladder
of Tyre
Cadasa
Gaulanitis
Batanea
Ecdippa
Gischala
Ptolemais
Chorazin
Bethsaida-Julias
Raphana
GALILEE
Capernaum
Cana
Magdala
Bosor
Asochis
Tiberias
Sea
Hippos
Dion?
Mediterranean
Sepphoris
of
Galilee
Gabae
Nazareth
Philoteria
Yarmuk
Auranitis
Plain
Mt. Tabor
Abila
Sea
of
Nain
Gadara
Capitolias
Dora
Esdraelon
Agrippina
Crocodilon
Arbela
Bostra
Caesarea
Scythopolis
DECAPOLIS
Narbata
Ginae
Pella
Salim
Aenon
Gerasa
SAMARIA
Jordan
Sebaste
(Samaria)
Mt. Ebal
Amathus
Apollonia
Mt. Gerizim
Sychar
Jabbok
Antipatris
Alexandrium
Joppa
Phasaelis
Gadara
Arimathea?
PEREA
Philadelphia
Gophna
Ephraim
Archelais
Lydda
Jericho
Betharamphtha
Jamnia
Cyprus
(Livias, Julias)
Emmaus
(Nicopolis)
Emmaus?
Esbus
Jerusalem
Bethany
Qumran
Azotus
Bethlehem
Essene community
Medeba
Hyrcania
JUDEA
Herodium
Ascalon
Marisa
Callirrhoe
Bethsura
Machaerus
Agrippias
Hebron
Gaza
Engaddi
Arnon
Raphia
IDUMEA
Masada
Areopolis
Bersabe
Malatha
Charachmoba
Elusa
NABATEA

Mediterranean

Sea

Plain of Sharon

Mt. Carmel

Phoenicia

Lake Asphaltitis (Dead Sea)

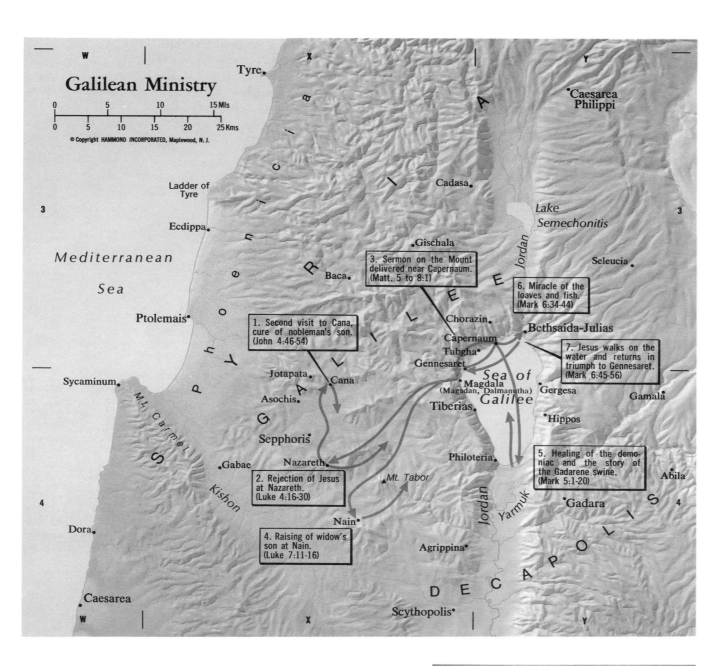

Galilean Ministry

0   5   10   15 Mls
0   5   10   15   20   25 Kms
© Copyright HAMMOND INCORPORATED, Maplewood, N. J.

1. Second visit to Cana, cure of nobleman's son. (John 4:46-54)

2. Rejection of Jesus at Nazareth. (Luke 4:16-30)

3. Sermon on the Mount delivered near Capernaum. (Matt. 5 to 8:1)

4. Raising of widow's son at Nain. (Luke 7:11-16)

5. Healing of the demoniac and the story of the Gadarene swine. (Mark 5:1-20)

6. Miracle of the loaves and fish. (Mark 6:34-44)

7. Jesus walks on the water and returns in triumph to Gennesaret. (Mark 6:45-56)

Tyre
Caesarea Philippi
Ladder of Tyre
Cadasa
Lake Semechonitis
Ecdippa
Seleucia
Mediterranean Sea
Gischala
Baca
Ptolemais
Chorazin
Capernaum
Bethsaida-Julias
Tabgha
Gennesaret
Sycaminum
Jotapata
Cana
Magdala (Magadan, Dalmanutha)
Sea of Galilee
Gergesa
Gamala
Asochis
Tiberias
Hippos
Mt. Carmel
Sepphoris
Gabae
Nazareth
Philoteria
Abila
Mt. Tabor
Gadara
Dora
Kishon
Nain
Jordan
Yarmuk
Caesarea
Agrippina
Scythopolis
PHOENICIA
GALILEE
DECAPOLIS

Above the waters of the Sea of Galilee the Church of the Beatitudes dominates the hill where tradition says Jesus preached the Sermon on the Mount.

The excavated synagogue at Capernaum (right) is later than the time of Jesus, but recalls that the Galilean Ministry was based in Capernaum, where Jesus spent much time teaching and healing in the synagogue.

The River Jordan near the Dead Sea, traditional site of Jesus' baptism.

Machaerus, where John the Baptist was put to death on orders of Herod Antipas.

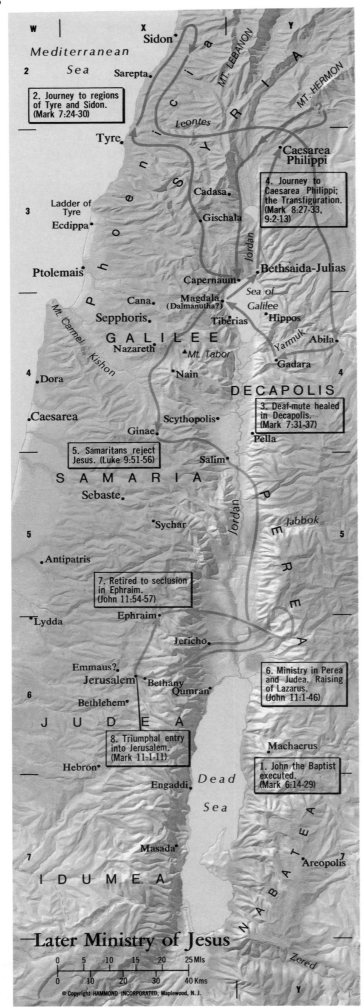

2. Journey to regions of Tyre and Sidon. (Mark 7:24-30)

4. Journey to Caesarea Philippi; the Transfiguration. (Mark 8:27-33, 9:2-13)

3. Deaf-mute healed in Decapolis. (Mark 7:31-37)

5. Samaritans reject Jesus. (Luke 9:51-56)

7. Retired to seclusion in Ephraim. (John 11:54-57)

6. Ministry in Perea and Judea. Raising of Lazarus. (John 11:1-46)

8. Triumphal entry into Jerusalem. (Mark 11:1-11)

1. John the Baptist executed. (Mark 6:14-29)

Later Ministry of Jesus

0 5 10 15 20 25 Mls
0 10 20 30 40 Kms
© Copyright HAMMOND INCORPORATED, Maplewood, N.J.

The Events of Passion Week
(According to the Synoptic Gospels)

	MATT.	MARK	LUKE
SUNDAY (Palm Sunday)			
Triumphal entry into Jerusalem	21:1-9	11:1-10	19:28-44
Visit to Temple and return to Bethany	21:10-17	11:11	19:45-46
MONDAY			
On the way to Jerusalem Jesus curses an unfruitful fig tree	21:18-19	11:12-14	
The Temple court cleansed		11:15-19	19:45-48
TUESDAY			
Returning to Jerusalem, Jesus explains the withering of the fig tree	21:20-22	11:20-26	
Jesus' authority is questioned	21:23-27	11:27-33	20:1-8
Teachings in the Temple	21:28-46; 22	12:1-37a	20:9-44
Condemnation of scribes and Pharisees	23:1-36	12:37b-40	20:45-47
Jesus in Temple treasury calls attention to widow's gift		12:41-44	21:1-4
Prediction of destruction of the Temple and the end of the World	24:1-44	13:1-37	21:5-38
WEDNESDAY			
Conspiracy against Jesus	26:1-5	14:1-2	22:1-2
Anointing at Bethany	26:6-13	14:1-9	
Judas agrees to betray Jesus	26:14-16	14:10-11	22:3-6
THURSDAY (Maundy Thursday)			
Jesus prepares to celebrate Passover	26:17-19	14:12-16	22:7-13
The Last Supper	26:20-29	14:17-25	22:14-38
Withdrawal to Gethsemane	26:30-46	14:26-42	22:39-46
Betrayal and arrest of Jesus	26:47-56	14:43-52	22:47-53
Jesus before Caiaphas and members of the Sanhedrin; Peter's denial	26:57-75	14:53-72	22:54-71
FRIDAY (Good Friday)			
Trial before Pilate; Judas' suicide	27:1-2	15:1-5	23:1-5
Jesus sent to Herod			23:6-16
Pilate imposes sentence of death	27:15-26	15:6-15	23:17-25
Jesus scourged and led to Golgotha	27:27-32	15:15-21	
Jesus' crucifixion and death	27:33-56	15:22-41	23:33-49
Jesus is buried	27:57-61	15:42-47	23:50-56
SATURDAY			
The guarded tomb	27:62-66		
SUNDAY (Easter)			
The empty tomb and the risen Christ	28:1-10	16:1-8	24:1-12

A modern church at ancient Bethany marks the traditional place where Jesus raised Lazarus from the dead (John 11:1-44).

Silver denarius of Tiberius, "tribute money" of Luke 20:21-26.

At Caesarea, residence of the Roman governors, archaeologists found this dedication stone with the only known inscriptional reference to Pontius Pilate.

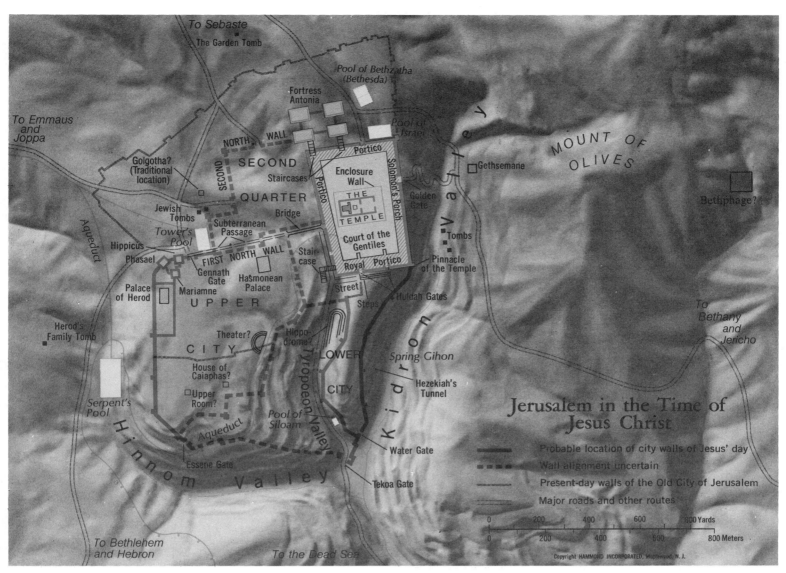

Jerusalem in the Time of Jesus Christ

To Sebaste
The Garden Tomb
Pool of Bethzatha (Bethesda)
Fortress Antonia
To Emmaus and Joppa
Pool of Israel
NORTH WALL
Portico
Golgotha? (Traditional location)
SECOND
Enclosure Wall
THE TEMPLE
MOUNT OF OLIVES
Staircases
Gethsemane
QUARTER
Solomon's Porch
Jewish Tombs
Bridge
Subterranean Passage
Court of the Gentiles
Golden Gate
Bethphage?
Tower's Pool
Hippicus
FIRST NORTH WALL
Staircase
Tombs
Phasael
Gennath Gate
Hasmonean Palace
Royal Portico
Pinnacle of the Temple
Aqueduct
Palace of Herod
Mariamne
Street
Huldah Gates
UPPER
Steps
Herod's Family Tomb
Theater?
CITY
Hippodrome
LOWER CITY
Spring Gihon
To Bethany and Jericho
House of Caiaphas?
Tyropoeon Valley
Hezekiah's Tunnel
Serpent's Pool
Upper Room?
Kidron Valley
Aqueduct
Pool of Siloam
Essene Gate
Hinnom Valley
Water Gate
Tekoa Gate
To Bethlehem and Hebron
To the Dead Sea

Probable location of city walls of Jesus' day
Wall alignment uncertain
Present-day walls of the Old City of Jerusalem
Major roads and other routes

0   200   400   600   800 Yards
0   200   400   600   800 Meters

Copyright HAMMOND INCORPORATED, Maplewood, N.J.

Today a mosque, the magnificent Dome of the Rock, occupies the platform where Herod's Temple stood in Jesus' day.

A model of Jerusalem shows the Temple platform and four towers of Fortress Antonia. The Pool of Bethzatha where Jesus healed the crippled man is in the foreground.

The Garden Tomb, a rock-cut tomb of the type in which Jesus was buried. North of Jerusalem, this quiet spot just outside the present north wall is a rival to the traditional site of the crucifixion and burial.

Judas' 30 pieces of silver may have been Tyrian shekels of this type.

"The Pavement" (courtyard) of the Fortress Antonia was possibly the place where Jesus was tried by Pilate. Today it is the crypt of a church and convent.

Theodotus synagogue inscription found on Mount Zion in Jerusalem. Some think this dedicatory inscription refers to the "Synagogue of the Freedmen" mentioned in Acts 6:9.

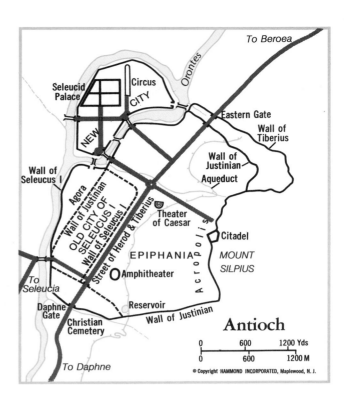

The Lion Gate in Jerusalem's east wall. Medieval Christian tradition locates the martyrdom of Stephen (Acts 7:58-60) nearby. Therefore Christians call this "St. Stephen's Gate."

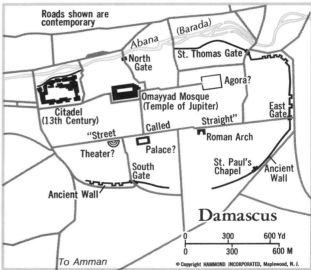

St. Paul's Chapel, Damascus. This is the traditional location of Paul's escape over the city wall (Acts 9:25).

The theater by the sea at Caesarea where in 10 B.C. Herod dedicated his splendid new city. Now restored, it is used for concerts.

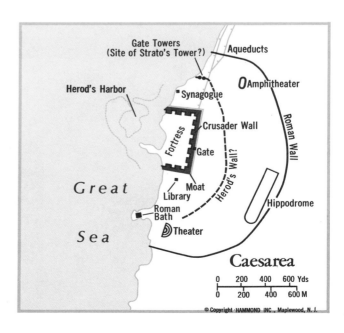

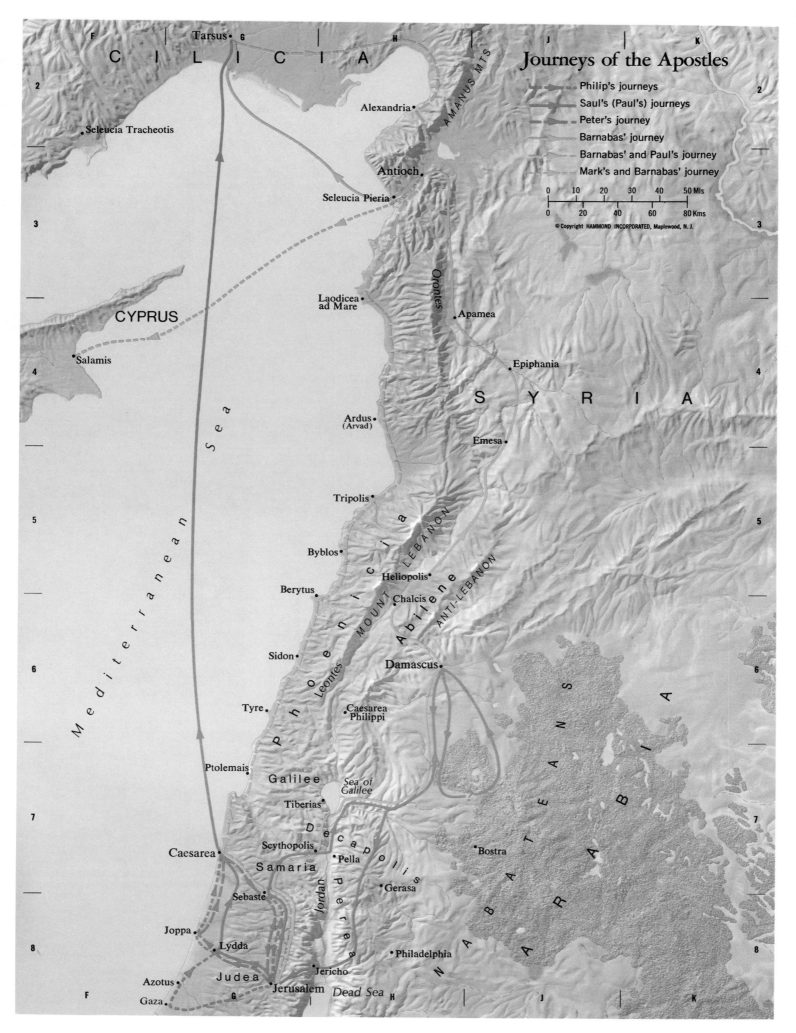

Journeys of the Apostles

- — — ► Philip's journeys
- ———— Saul's (Paul's) journeys
- ━━━━━ Peter's journey
- - - - - Barnabas' journey
- ———— Barnabas' and Paul's journey
- - - - - Mark's and Barnabas' journey

0 10 20 30 40 50 Mls
0 20 40 60 80 Kms

© Copyright HAMMOND INCORPORATED, Maplewood, N. J.

CILICIA

Tarsus

Seleucia Tracheotis

Alexandria

AMANUS MTS

Antioch

Seleucia Pieria

CYPRUS

Salamis

Laodicea ad Mare

Apamea

Orontes

SYRIA

Epiphania

Ardus (Arvad)

Emesa

Tripolis

LEBANON

Byblos

Heliopolis

Abilene

ANTI-LEBANON

Berytus

Chalcis

Sidon

Leontes

Damascus

Tyre

Caesarea Philippi

Phoenicia

Mediterranean Sea

Ptolemais

Galilee

Sea of Galilee

Tiberias

Decapolis

NABATEAN ARABIA

Caesarea

Scythopolis

Samaria

Pella

Bostra

Gerasa

Jordan

Perea

Sebaste

Joppa

Philadelphia

Lydda

Jericho

Azotus

Judea

Jerusalem

Dead Sea

Gaza

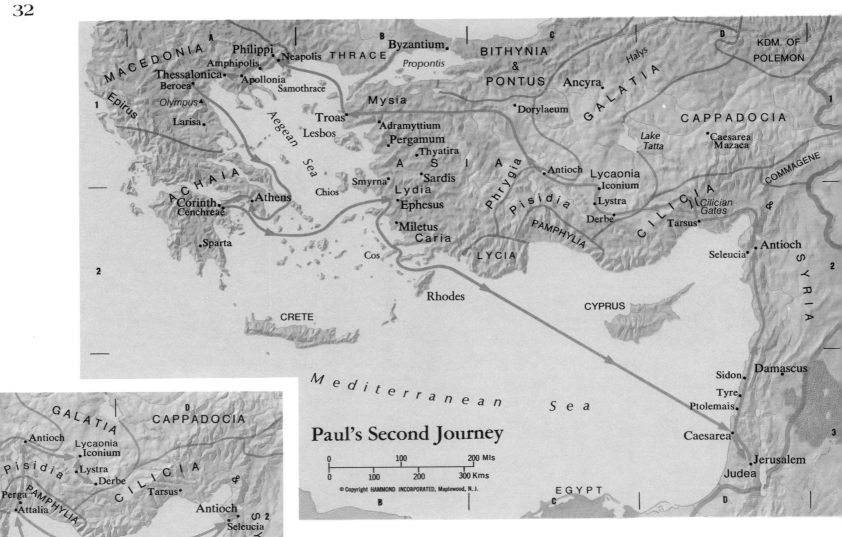

Paul's Second Journey

0   100   200 MIs
0   100   200   300 Kms
© Copyright HAMMOND INCORPORATED, Maplewood, N.J.

MACEDONIA
Philippi • Neapolis THRACE   Byzantium •
Amphipolis   Propontis   BITHYNIA
Thessalonica •   • Apollonia   & PONTUS   Ancyra   KDM. OF POLEMON
Beroea   Samothrace   GALATIA
Olympus ▲   • Dorylaeum   CAPPADOCIA
Larisa •   Troas •   Phrygia
                        Adramyttium •   • Antioch   Lake Tatta   • Caesarea Mazaca
           Aegean   Lesbos   Pergamum •   A S I A   Lycaonia   COMMAGENE
ACHAIA   Sea   Thyatira •   • Iconium
           Chios   Smyrna • Sardis •   Pisidia • Lystra   Cilician Gates
• Corinth Athens • Lydia Ephesus •   Derbe •   Tarsus • CILICIA
Cenchreae •   Miletus •   Caria   PAMPHYLIA   Seleucia • • Antioch
                                              LYCIA   SYRIA
• Sparta   Cos   Sidon • Damascus
                Rhodes   CYPRUS   Tyre •
                                                              Ptolemais •
        CRETE   Caesarea •   Jerusalem
     M e d i t e r r a n e a n   S e a   Judea
                                        EGYPT

Temple of Apollo, Corinth. Only 7 of the 38 columns seen by Paul are now standing.

Artemis was the chief deity of Ephesus. Paul's attack on the worship of this goddess provoked a riot (Acts 19:23f.).

Paul's First Journey

GALATIA   CAPPADOCIA
• Antioch   Lycaonia
Pisidia   Iconium
        • Lystra
        Derbe •   CILICIA
Perga • PAMPHYLIA Tarsus •
• Attalia   Antioch
              Seleucia
        CYPRUS   • Salamis
        Paphos •
              Damascus •
              • Caesarea
              Jerusalem
              Judea

0   100   200 MIs
0   100   200   300 Kms
© Copyright HAMMOND INCORPORATED, Maplewood, N.J.

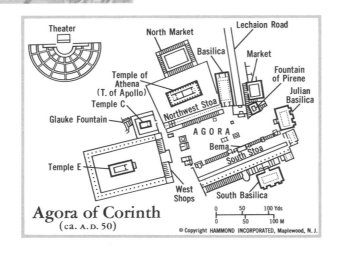

Agora of Corinth
(ca. A.D. 50)

Theater, North Market, Basilica, Lechaion Road, Market, Fountain of Pirene, Temple of Athena (T. of Apollo), Julian Basilica, Temple C, Northwest Stoa, Glauke Fountain, AGORA, Bema, South Stoa, Temple E, West Shops, South Basilica

0 50 100 Yds
0 50 100 M
© Copyright HAMMOND INCORPORATED, Maplewood, N.J.

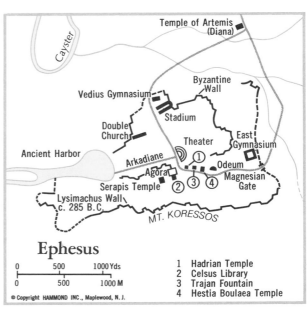

Ephesus

Cayster, Temple of Artemis (Diana), Vedius Gymnasium, Byzantine Wall, Stadium, Double Church, Theater, East Gymnasium, Ancient Harbor, Arkadiane, Odeum, Agora, Serapis Temple, Magnesian Gate, Lysimachus Wall c. 285 B.C., MT. KORESSOS

0   500   1000 Yds
0   500   1000 M
© Copyright HAMMOND INC., Maplewood, N.J.

1 Hadrian Temple
2 Celsus Library
3 Trajan Fountain
4 Hestia Boulaea Temple

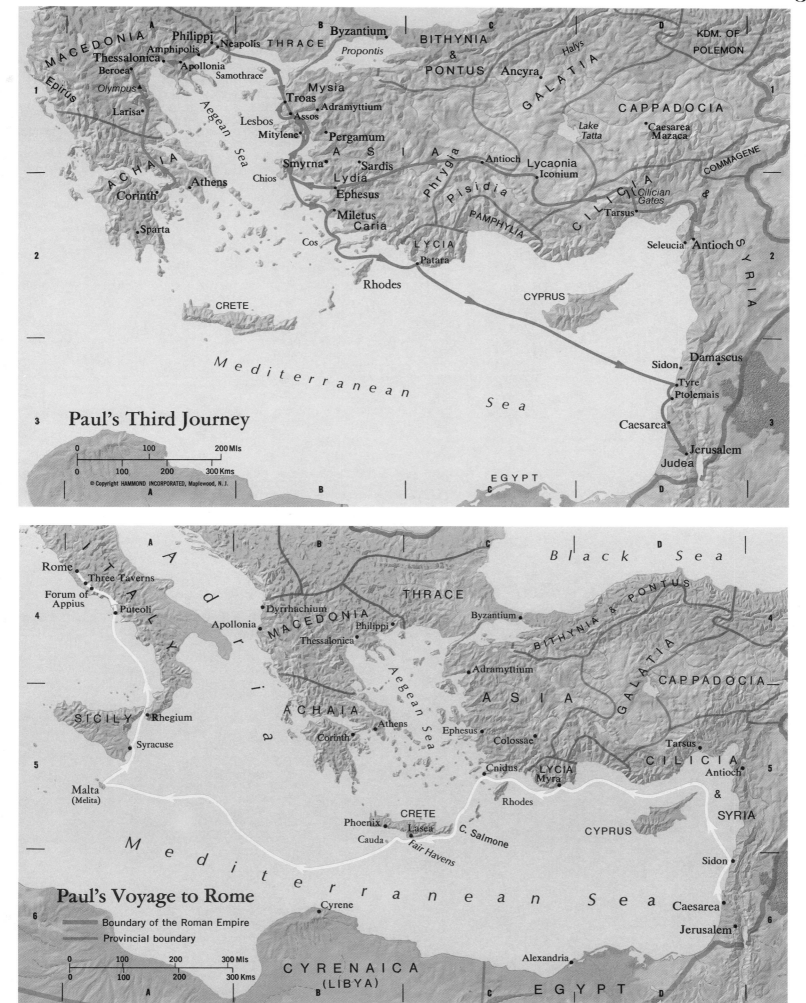

Paul's Third Journey

MACEDONIA · Philippi · Neapolis · THRACE · Byzantium · *Propontis* · BITHYNIA & PONTUS · Ancyra · *Halys* · KDM. OF POLEMON
Amphipolis · Apollonia · Samothrace · GALATIA · CAPPADOCIA
Thessalonica · Beroea · Olympus ▲ · Larisa · Mysia · Troas · Assos · Adramyttium · Lesbos · Mitylene · Pergamum · Caesarea Mazaca
Aegean Sea · ASIA · Phrygia · Antioch · Lycaonia · Iconium · COMMAGENE
Epirus · ACHAIA · Athens · Chios · Smyrna · Sardis · Lydia · Ephesus · Pisidia · CILICIA · Cilician Gates · Tarsus · & · SYRIA
Corinth · Miletus · Caria · PAMPHYLIA · Seleucia · Antioch
Sparta · Cos · LYCIA · Patara · Sidon · Damascus
Rhodes · CYPRUS · Tyre · Ptolemais
CRETE · Caesarea
Mediterranean Sea · Jerusalem · Judea
EGYPT

Scale: 0 — 100 — 200 Mls · 0 — 100 — 200 — 300 Kms
© Copyright HAMMOND INCORPORATED, Maplewood, N.J.

Paul's Voyage to Rome

Rome · Three Taverns · ITALY · *Black Sea*
Forum of Appius · Puteoli · Apollonia · Dyrrhachium · MACEDONIA · THRACE · Byzantium · BITHYNIA & PONTUS
Thessalonica · Philippi · Adramyttium · GALATIA · CAPPADOCIA
Adria · *Aegean Sea* · ASIA
SICILY · Rhegium · ACHAIA · Athens · Ephesus · Colossae · Tarsus · CILICIA
Syracuse · Corinth · Cnidus · LYCIA · Myra · Antioch · & · SYRIA
Malta (Melita) · CRETE · Rhodes · CYPRUS
Phoenix · Lasea · C. Salmone · Sidon
Cauda · Fair Havens
Mediterranean Sea · Caesarea
Cyrene · Jerusalem
CYRENAICA (LIBYA) · Alexandria · EGYPT

— Boundary of the Roman Empire
— Provincial boundary

Scale: 0 — 100 — 200 — 300 Mls · 0 — 100 — 200 — 300 Kms

34

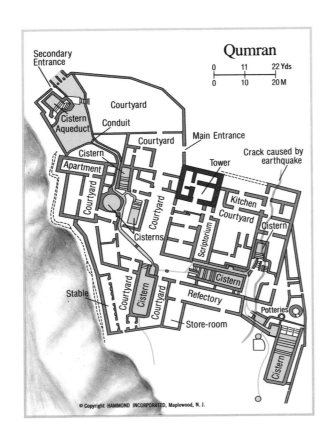

Qumran

0 — 11 — 22 Yds
0 — 10 — 20 M

Secondary Entrance
Cistern
Aqueduct
Conduit
Courtyard
Courtyard
Main Entrance
Courtyard
Crack caused by earthquake
Tower
Apartment
Cistern
Courtyard
Kitchen
Courtyard
Scriptorium
Courtyard
Cistern
Cisterns
Cistern
Courtyard
Stable
Courtyard
Cistern
Refectory
Courtyard
Potteries
Store-room
Cistern

© Copyright HAMMOND INCORPORATED, Maplewood, N.J.

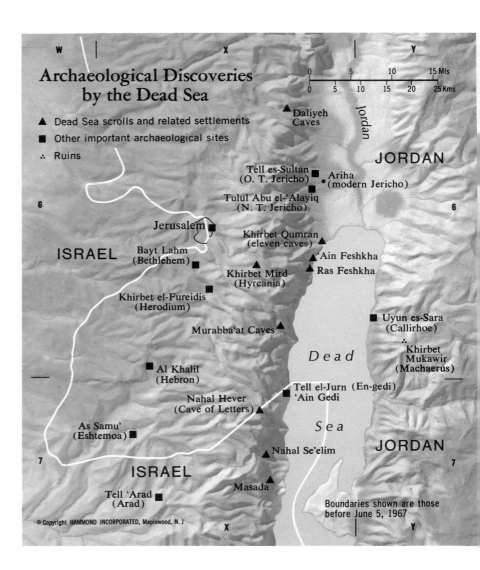

Archaeological Discoveries by the Dead Sea

0 — 5 — 10 — 15 Mls
0 — 5 — 10 — 15 — 20 — 25 Kms

▲ Dead Sea scrolls and related settlements
■ Other important archaeological sites
∴ Ruins

W — X — Y

JORDAN

Daliyeh Caves

Tell es-Sultan (O. T. Jericho)
Ariha (modern Jericho)
Tulul Abu el-'Alayiq (N. T. Jericho)

Jerusalem
Khirbet Qumran (eleven caves)
'Ain Feshkha
Ras Feshkha

ISRAEL
Bayt Lahm (Bethlehem)
Khirbet Mird (Hyrcania)

Khirbet el-Fureidis (Herodium)

Uyun es-Sara (Callirhoe)

Murabba'at Caves

Dead

Khirbet Mukawir (Machaerus)

Al Khalil (Hebron)

Tell el-Jurn (En-gedi) 'Ain Gedi

Nahal Hever (Cave of Letters)

Sea

JORDAN

As Samu' (Eshtemoa)

Nahal Se'elim

ISRAEL

Masada

Tell 'Arad (Arad)

Boundaries shown are those before June 5, 1967

© Copyright HAMMOND INCORPORATED, Maplewood, N.J

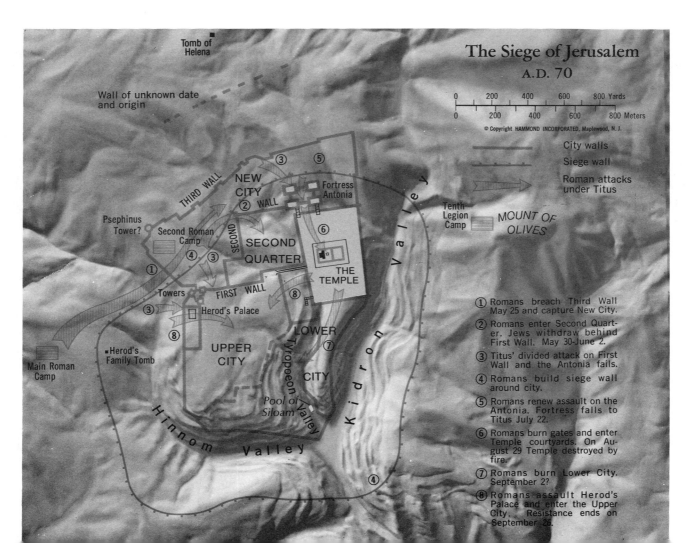

The Siege of Jerusalem
A.D. 70

0 — 200 — 400 — 600 — 800 Yards
0 — 200 — 400 — 600 — 800 Meters

© Copyright HAMMOND INCORPORATED, Maplewood, N.J.

City walls
Siege wall
Roman attacks under Titus

Tomb of Helena
Wall of unknown date and origin

THIRD WALL
NEW CITY
WALL
Fortress Antonia

Psephinus Tower?
Second Roman Camp
SECOND
SECOND QUARTER
THE TEMPLE

Tenth Legion Camp
MOUNT OF OLIVES

Towers
FIRST WALL
Herod's Palace

LOWER CITY

Tyropoeon Valley

Kidron Valley

Main Roman Camp
Herod's Family Tomb

UPPER CITY

Pool of Siloam

Hinnom Valley

① Romans breach Third Wall May 25 and capture New City.
② Romans enter Second Quarter. Jews withdraw behind First Wall. May 30-June 2.
③ Titus' divided attack on First Wall and the Antonia fails.
④ Romans build siege wall around city.
⑤ Romans renew assault on the Antonia. Fortress falls to Titus July 22.
⑥ Romans burn gates and enter Temple courtyards. On August 29 Temple destroyed by fire.
⑦ Romans burn Lower City. September 2?
⑧ Romans assault Herod's Palace and enter the Upper City. Resistance ends on September 26.

Cave Four (center) at Qumran, in which a wealth of precious scrolls were found.

Masada, the impregnable rock fortress of Herod the Great, was the last stronghold of the Jews in the revolt against Rome.

Masada

Labels on Masada map:
Lower Aqueduct
Cisterns
Upper Aqueduct
Water Gate
Three-tiered Northern Palace
Large Bathhouse
Admin. Bldg.
Storerooms
Cisterns
Synagogue
Gate
Snake Path
Roman Siege Ramp
Large Dwelling
Western Gate
Western Palace
Small Palaces
Ritual Bath
Southern Water Gate
Cistern
Southern Bastion
Valley

0   50   100   150 Yds
0   50   100   150 M
Copyright HAMMOND INC., Maplewood, N.J.

The First Jewish Revolt

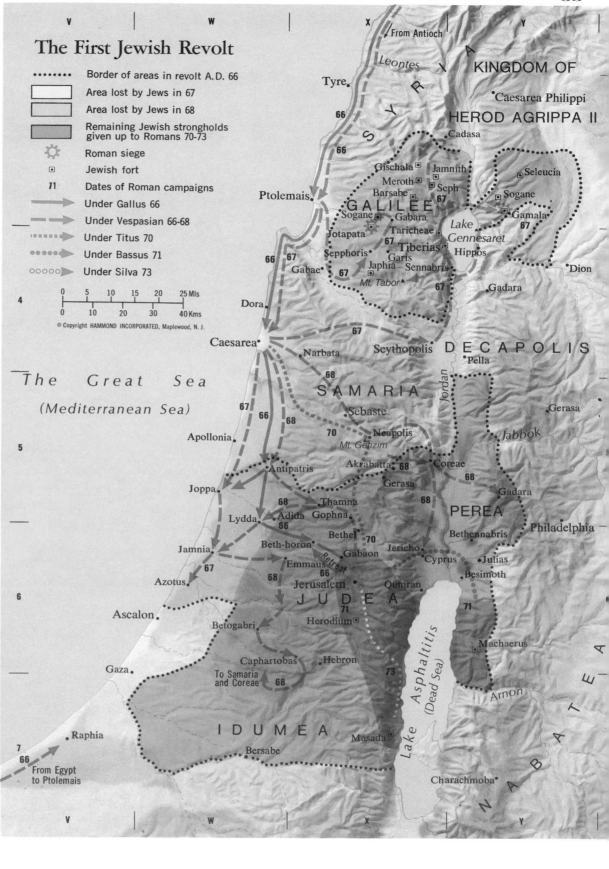

Legend:
- •••••• Border of areas in revolt A.D. 66
- Area lost by Jews in 67
- Area lost by Jews in 68
- Remaining Jewish strongholds given up to Romans 70-73
- ☼ Roman siege
- ▣ Jewish fort
- *11* Dates of Roman campaigns
- → Under Gallus 66
- --→ Under Vespasian 66-68
- ····→ Under Titus 70
- •••→ Under Bassus 71
- ○○○→ Under Silva 73

0   5   10   15   20   25 Mls
0   10   20   30   40 Kms
© Copyright HAMMOND INCORPORATED, Maplewood, N.J.

Map labels:
From Antioch
Leontes
Tyre
KINGDOM OF
Caesarea Philippi
HEROD AGRIPPA II
Cadasa
Gischala
Jamnith
Seleucia
Meroth
Seph
Barsabe
Sogane
GALILEE
Sogane
Gabara
Gamala
Jotapata
Taricheae
Lake Gennesaret
Ptolemais
Sepphoris
Tiberias
Hippos
Garis
Gabae
Japhia
Sennabris
Dion
Mt. Tabor
Dora
Gadara
Caesarea
Scythopolis
DECAPOLIS
Narbata
Pella
Jordan
SAMARIA
Gerasa
The Great Sea
(Mediterranean Sea)
Sebaste
Neapolis
Mt. Gerizim
Jabbok
Apollonia
Akrabatta
Coreae
Antipatris
Gerasa
Gadara
Joppa
Thamna
PEREA
Lydda
Adida
Gophna
Philadelphia
Bethel
Jamnia
Beth-horon
Gabaon
Jericho
Bethennabris
Emmaus
Cyprus
Julias
Azotus
Jerusalem
Qumran
Besimoth
JUDEA
Ascalon
Herodium
Lake Asphaltitis (Dead Sea)
Betogabri
Machaerus
Gaza
Caphartobas
Hebron
To Samaria and Coreae
IDUMEA
Masada
Raphia
Bersabe
From Egypt to Ptolemais
Charachmoba
Arnon
NABATEA

Silver shekel from "the year two," the second year of the Revolt, A.D. 67.

Roman "Judaea Capta" coins. Above are Vespasian and Titus. Sestertius, right, shows a captive Jewess.

GERMANIA

Cologne
Trier
Rhine

GAUL

Danube

Lugdunum
(Lyons)
Vienne

ILLYRICUM
Salona

DAC

SPAIN

Astorga
Leon

Saragossa

ITALY

MOE

Merida

Rome
Ostia
Antium
Puteoli

MACEDONIA
Philippi

THF

Hispalis
Corduba

Beroea
Thessalonica
Larissa

Mediterranean

Sicily

Nicopolis

ACHAIA

MAURETANIA

Sitifi
Cirta
Thuburba
Carthage
Lambesis
Madaurus
Uthina
Numidia
Hadrumetum
Thysdrus

Syracuse

Patrae
Corinth
Athens

Sparta

AFRICA

Gortyna

The Spread of Christianity

- The Seven Churches of Asia (Rev. 1-3)
- City with Christian church recorded in second century

Regions known to contain Christians by A.D. 185
(the time of Irenaeus)

Boundary of the Roman empire
for most of second century

Temporarily controlled by Rome

Cyrene

CYRENAICA

| 0 | 100 | 200 | 300 | 400 | 500Mls |
| 0 | 200 | 400 | 600 | 800Kms |

© Copyright HAMMOND INCORPORATED, Maplewood, N.J.

The Flavian Amphitheater (Colosseum) in
Rome, where many Christians were martyred.

St. Paul's-Outside-the-Walls, Rome,
traditional site of the tomb of Paul.

Constantine made Christianity
a "legal religion" in A.D. 311.

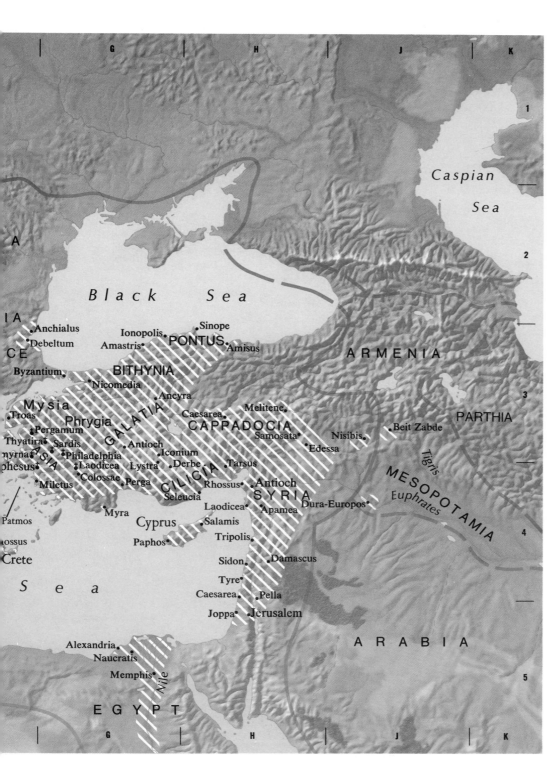

Black Sea

Caspian Sea

Anchialus
Debeltum
Ionopolis
Amastris
Sinope
PONTUS
Amisus
Byzantium
BITHYNIA
Nicomedia
Ancyra
ARMENIA
Mysia
Troas
Phrygia
GALATIA
Caesarea
Melitene
CAPPADOCIA
PARTHIA
Pergamum
Thyatira
Sardis
ASIA
Antioch
Iconium
Samosata
Nisibis
Beit Zabde
Philadelphia
Lystra
Derbe
Tarsus
Edessa
myrna
Laodicea
CILICIA
Rhossus
Antioch
MESOPOTAMIA
phesus
Colossae
Perga
SYRIA
Dura-Europos
Euphrates
Miletus
Seleucia
Laodicea
Apamea
Tigris
Myra
Cyprus
Salamis
Patmos
Paphos
Tripolis
ossus
Sidon
Damascus
Crete
Tyre
Caesarea
Pella
Sea
Joppa
Jerusalem
ARABIA
Alexandria
Naucratis
Memphis
Nile
EGYPT

The Seven Churches of Asia Minor

Byzantium
Chalcedon
Samothrace
Propontis
Cyzicus
Nicaea
Imbros
Abydos
Mysia
Prusa
Ilium
Troas (Alexandria)
Assos
Adramyttium
Lesbos
Mitylene
Pergamum
Aegean
Thyatria
Chios
Smyrna
Sardis
ASIA
Sea
Metropolis
Lydia
Philadelphia
Claros
Ephesus
Hierapolis
Samos
Panionium
Tralles
Magnesia
Laodicea
Delos
Trogyllium
Priene
Aphrodisias
Colossae
Patmos
Didyma
Miletus
Naxos
Caria
Halicarnassus
Cos
LYCIA
Cnidus
Xanthus
Patara
Rhodes

† The Seven Churches
  of Asia   (Rev. 1-3)
— Principal roads

0   50   100 Mls
0   100 Kms

© Copyright HAMMOND INC., Maplewood, N.J.

Chalice of Antioch shows Christ and apostles. It dates from 4th or 5th century A.D.

Patmos, where The Revelation to St. John the Divine, the last book in the New Testament, was written.

Papyrus fragment of the Gospel of Matthew from Oxyrhynchus, Egypt.

The four-spouted oil lamp (top)
is from Patriarchal times;
the Herodian lamp (bottom)
is typical of Jesus' day.

The Moabite Stone, found in 1868
at Mesha's capital. Carved about
840-820 B.C., it tells of the events of
2 Kings 3:4-27 and their aftermath
from a Moabite point of view.

The mound of Tell el-Hesi. One of
the first sites to be excavated in
Palestine, it is thought to be
Biblical Eglon, a Canaanite royal
city taken by Joshua (Joshua 10).

Archaeological Sites
in Israel and Jordan

■ Principal excavated sites
T, Tel, Tell: city site or mound
Kh, Khirbet: ruin

0 5 10 15 20 25 30 Mls
0 10 20 30 40 50 Kms

© Copyright by HAMMOND INC., Maplewood, N.J.

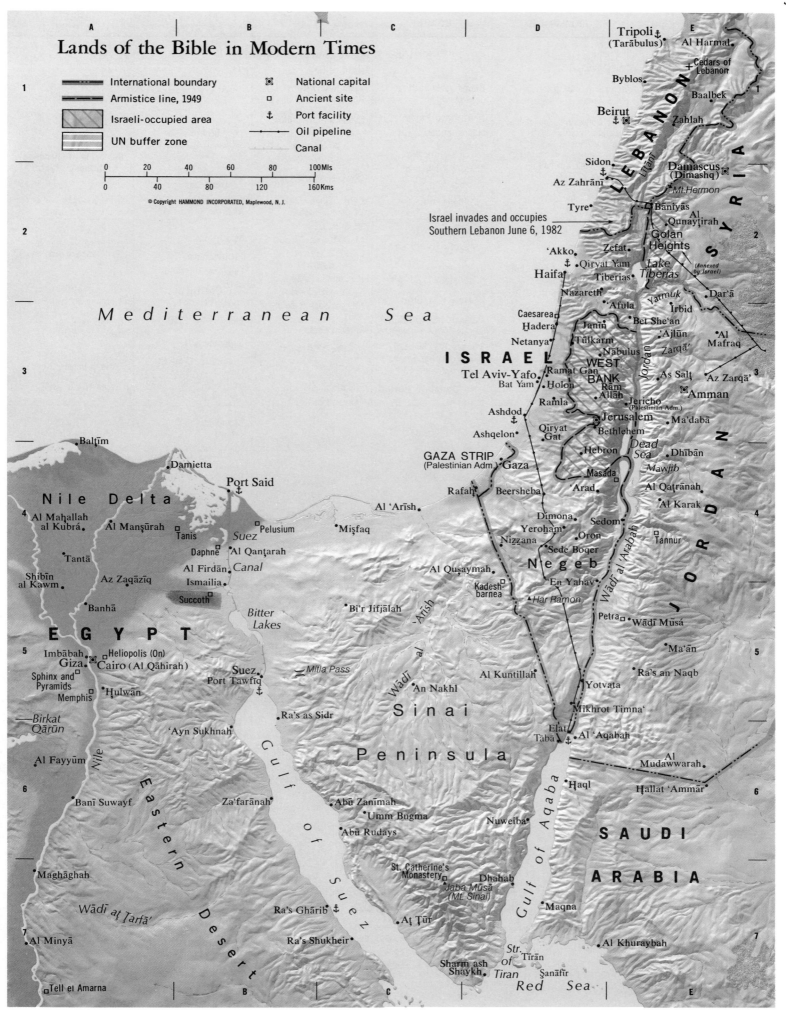

Lands of the Bible in Modern Times

─·─·─ International boundary	⊡ National capital
─··─··─ Armistice line, 1949	☐ Ancient site
▨ Israeli-occupied area	⚓ Port facility
▤ UN buffer zone	•─•─• Oil pipeline
	Canal

0 20 40 60 80 100 Mls
0 40 80 120 160 Kms

© Copyright HAMMOND INCORPORATED, Maplewood, N.J.

Israel invades and occupies
Southern Lebanon June 6, 1982

Mediterranean Sea

LEBANON

Tripoli (Tarābulus) ‡
Al Harmal
Cedars of Lebanon +
Byblos
Baalbek
Beirut ‡⊡
Zahlah
Sidon ‡
Damascus (Dimashq) ⊡
Az Zahrānī
Mt. Hermon
Tyre
Bāniyās
Al Qunayţirah
Golan Heights
(Annexed by Israel)
'Akko ⚓
Zefat
Qiryat Yam
Tiberias
Lake Tiberias
Haifa
Nazareth
Dar'ā
Afula
Yarmuk
Irbid
Caesarea
Janīn
Bet She'an
Hadera
Tūlkarm
'Ajlūn
Al Mafraq
Netanya
Nābulus
Zarqā'
ISRAEL
WEST BANK
Tel Aviv-Yafo
Ramat Gan
As Salţ
Az Zarqā'
Bat Yam
Holon
Rām Allāh
Jordan
Amman ⊡
Ramla
Jericho (Palestinian Adm.)
Ashdod ⚓
Jerusalem ⊡
Ma'daba
Qiryat Gat
Bethlehem
Ashqelon
Hebron
Dead Sea
Dhībān
GAZA STRIP
(Palestinian Adm.)
Gaza
Masada ☐
Mawjib
Rafah
Beersheba
Arad
Al Qaţrānah
Al 'Arīsh
Dimona
Sedom
Al Karak
Miṣfaq
Yeroham
Oron
Tannur ☐
Nizzana
Negeb
Al Quşaymah
Sede Boqer
Wādī al 'Arabah
Kadesh-barnea
En Yahav
Petra ☐
Wādī Mūsā
Bi'r Jifjālah
Har Ramon
Ma'ān
'Arīsh
Ra's an Naqb

Nile Delta
Balţīm
Damietta
Port Said ‡
Al Mahallah al Kubrá
Al Manşūrah
Tanis ☐
Suez
Pelusium ☐
Tanţā
Daphne ☐
Al Qanţarah
Shibīn al Kawm
Al Firdān
Canal
Az Zaqāzīq
Ismailia
Banhā
Succoth ☐
EGYPT
Bitter Lakes
Imbābah
Heliopolis (On) ☐
Giza ☐
Cairo (Al Qāhirah) ⊡
Sphinx and Pyramids
Memphis ☐
Ḥulwān
Suez
Port Tawfīq ‡
Mitla Pass
Wādī al 'Arīsh
An Nakhl
Al Kuntillah
Yotvata
Birkat Qārūn
Al Fayyūm
Ra's as Sidr
Sinai
Mikhrot Timna'
'Ayn Sukhnah
Elat
Tābā ‡
Al 'Aqabah
Nile
Peninsula
Al Mudawwarah
Banī Suwayf
Za'farānah
Abū Zanimah
Gulf of Aqaba
Ḥaql
Ḥallat 'Ammār
Umm Bugma
Nuweiba
Abū Rudays
SAUDI
Maghāghah
St. Catherine's Monastery
Dhahab
Jaba Mūsā (Mt. Sinai)
Maqna
ARABIA
Wādī aṭ Ţarfā'
Ra's Ghārib ‡
Aţ Ţūr
Al Minyā
Ra's Shukheir
Sharm ash Shaykh
Str. of Tiran
Ṣanāfir
Al Khuraybah
Tell el Amarna ☐
Red Sea

Eastern Desert
Gulf of Suez

SYRIA
JORDAN

Time Chart of Bible History

DATE	PALESTINE	EGYPT	MESOPOTAMIA & PERSIA	ANATOLIA & SYRIA	GREECE & ROME
4000 BC	Neolithic culture (Jericho) Ghassulian culture c.3500 The Canaanites, a Semitic people, were ancestral to the Phoenicians Early Bronze urban culture c.3300 Amorite invasions c.2500-2300	— First use of metal: copper and bronze — Hieroglyphic writing developed **Archaic Period** Menes unifies Egypt **Old Kingdom** The Great Pyramids at Gizeh c.2550 Old Kingdom falls	Halaf culture Cuneiform writing developed Sumerian city states c.2800-2360 **Akkadian Empire** Sargon I 2360-2305 Gutian kings Ur dominance	Early Bronze cities Byblos, Troy, Ugarit Syria under Akkadian Empire Hittites enter Anatolia	Beginning of Minoan civilization on Crete Greeks invade Balkan peninsula
2000 BC	Egypt controls Canaan Abraham — oral tradition Israelite sojourn in Egypt Battle of Megiddo 1468 Amarna letters c.1370-1353 The Exodus c.1290 Israelite invasion Philistine penetration Kdm. of Saul c.1020-1000	**Middle Kingdom** Hyksos invaders from Asia c.1720-1550 **New Kingdom** Akhenaton 1370-1353 Tutankhamen 1353-1344 Ramses II 1290-1224 Ramses III defeats Sea Peoples c.1170 **Late Dynastic Period**	Ur falls c.1950 **Isin-Larsa Period** **Old Babylonian Empire** Hammurabi 1728-1686 **Kassite Period** Hittites sack Babylon 1531 Mitanni Kdm. **Rise of Assyria** Shalmaneser I Tiglath-pileser I 1115-1078	Amorite invasions Hittites intro. Iron Labarnas I c.1600 **Old Hittite Kingdom** Mursilis I c.1540 Suppilullumas **Hittite Empire** Battle of Kedesh 1296 Sack of Troy 1192	**Minoan Sea Empire** Mycenae shaft graves Cretan palaces destroyed c.1400 Dorians invade Greece Trojan War c.1200
1000 BC	**United Kingdom** David c.1000-961 Solomon c.961-922 First Temple completed c.950 **Divided Kingdom** Rehoboam & Jeroboam I Omri dynasty 876-842 Samaria founded c.875 Jehu dynasty 842-745	Period of decline Shishak c.935-914 Libyan dynasties 950-710	**Assyrian Empire** Asshurnasirpal II 883-859 Shalmaneser III 859-824 Adad-nirari III 807-782	Arameans flood into Syria Hiram of Tyre 969-936 Damascus city state Ben-hadad II Battle of Qarqar 853 Phoenicians found Carthage 814	Decline of Aegean Bronze Age civilization Latins settle in central Italy
800 BC / 600 BC	Israel resurgence under Jeroboam II 786-746 Amos, Hosea Fall of Samaria and exile of Israel 722/721 Hezekiah of Judah 715-687/6 Isaiah Micah Judah resurgence under Josiah 640-609 Jeremiah	Nubian dynasties 715-663 Egypt under Assyrian rule 671-652 Thebes sacked 663 Neco II 609-593	Tiglath-pileser III 745-727 Sargon II 722-705 Sennacherib 705-681 Asshurbanapal 669-633 Rise of Babylon under Nabopolassar Fall of Nineveh to Medes and Babylonians 612	Phrygian Kdm. Midas c.715 Lydian Kdm. Gyges of Lydia 680-652	First Olympics 776 Legendary founding of Rome 753 Etruscan period Homer Draco codifies Athenian law 621

Kings of Judah and Israel

JUDAH	ISRAEL	JUDAH	ISRAEL
Rehoboam 922-915	922-901 Jeroboam I	Jotham 750-735	746-745 Zechariah
Abijah 915-913	901-900 Nadab		745 Shallum
Asa 913-873	900-877 Baasha		745-738 Menahem
	877-876 Elah		738-737 Pekahiah
	876 Zimri	Ahaz 735-715	737-732 Pekah
Jehoshaphat 873-849	876-869 Omri		732-724 Hoshea
	869-850 Ahab	Hezekiah 715-687/6	722/721 Fall of Samaria
	850-849 Ahaziah	Manasseh 687/6-642	
Jehoram 849-842	849-842 Jehoram	Amon 642-640	
Ahaziah 842	842-815 Jehu	Josiah 640-609	
Athaliah 842-837		Jehoahaz 609	
Joash 837-800	815-801 Jehoahaz	Jehoiakim 609-598	
Amaziah 800-783	801-786 Jehoash	Jehoiachin 598-597	
Uzziah 783-742	786-746 Jeroboam II	Zedekiah 597-587	

Fall of Jerusalem 587

DATE	PALESTINE	EGYPT	MESOPOTAMIA & PERSIA	ANATOLIA & SYRIA	GREECE & ROME
600 BC	Destruction of Jerusalem and exile of Judah 587 Ezekiel **Babylonian Captivity** Edict of Cyrus allows return of Jews 538 Zerubbabel Temple rebuilt 520-515 **Persian Period** Ezra's mission 458?? Nehemiah comes to Judah 445 (440?)	Egypt under Persian rule 525-401 Unsuccessful revolt Return to native rule	**New Babylonian Empire** Nebuchadnezzar II 605-562 **Persian Empire** Cyrus 550-530 Babylon falls 539 Cambyses 530-522 Darius I 522-486 Xerxes I 486-465 Artaxerxes I Darius II 433-404	Syria and Anatolia under Persian rule Phoenicians provide fleet for Persian attacks on Greece	Solon's judicial reforms c.590 Rome ruled by Etruscan kings Roman Republic established 509 Persian Wars 499-479 Thermopylae-Salamis 480 Pericles 461-429 Herodotus
400 BC	Ezra's mission 398? Palestine passes under Alexander's rule and Hellenization begins 332 Ptolemaic Egyptian rule 312	Persian rule 342-332 Alexander conquers Egypt 332 Ptolemy I 323-284 **Ptolemaic Kingdom** Alexandrian Jews translate Pentateuch into Greek Ptolemy V 203-181	Artaxerxes III 358-338 Alexander invades Persia 331 Seleucid rule Parthians and Bactrians gain independence c.250	Alexander takes Tyre 332 Seleucid rule Seleucus I 312-280 **Seleucid Empire** Antiochus I 280-261 Seleucus II 246-226 Antiochus III (The Great) 223-187	Socrates' death Sack of Rome by Gauls Philip II of Macedon Alexander the Great 336-323 **Alexander's Empire** Wars of the Diodochi 1st and 2nd Punic Wars Hannibal in Italy 218
200 BC	Palestine comes under Seleucid Syrian control 198 **Maccabean Period** Judas Maccabeus leads revolt of Jews 166-160 Temple rededicated 164 Jonathan 160-142 Simon 142-134 John Hyrcanus I 134-104 Aristobulus I 104-103	Ptolemy VI 181-146 Antiochus IV campaigns in Egypt Ptolemy VII 146-116	**Parthian Empire** Mithridates I 171-138 Mithridates II 124-88	Battle of Magnesia 190 Antiochus IV (Epiphanes) 175-163 Antiochus V 163-162 Demetrius I 162-150 Demetrius II 145-139 Tyre independent	Spain annexed by Rome **Empire of the Roman Republic** 3rd Punic War Romans destroy Carthage and Corinth 146 Reforms of the Gracchi
100 BC **50 BC**	Alexander Jannaeus 103-76 Alexandra 76-67 Aristobulus II 67-63 Pompey takes Jerusalem for Rome 63 Hyrcanus II, high priest 63-40 Antipater governor 55	Ptolemy VIII 116-81 Ptolemy XI 80-81 Cleopatra VII 51-30	Tigranes of Armenia Phrates III 70-57 Orodes I 57-38 War with Rome 55-38 Crassus defeated	Mithridatic Wars Antiochus XIII 68-67 Anatolia and Syria under Roman control	Sulla dictator 82-79 1st Triumvirate Pompey's campaigns in Asia 66-63 Caesar's Gallic Wars 58-51

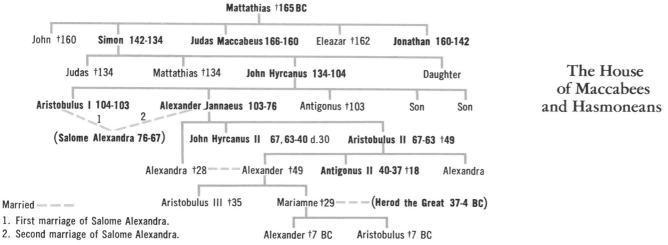

The House
of Maccabees
and Hasmoneans

Mattathias †165 BC

John †160   Simon 142-134   Judas Maccabeus 166-160   Eleazar †162   Jonathan 160-142

Judas †134   Mattathias †134   John Hyrcanus 134-104   Daughter

Aristobulus I 104-103   Alexander Jannaeus 103-76   Antigonus †103   Son   Son

1   2

(Salome Alexandra 76-67)   John Hyrcanus II 67, 63-40 d.30   Aristobulus II 67-63 †49

Alexandra †28 - - - Alexander †49   Antigonus II 40-37 †18   Alexandra

Aristobulus III †35   Mariamne †29 - - - (Herod the Great 37-4 BC)

Alexander †7 BC   Aristobulus †7 BC

Married - - -
1. First marriage of Salome Alexandra.
2. Second marriage of Salome Alexandra.

Time Chart of Bible History, Continued

DATE	PALESTINE	THE WEST	THE EAST
50 BC	**Roman Rule** Caesar in Judea 47 Parthian invasion 40 Antigonus 40-37 Herod the Great 37-4 BC Herod's Temple begun 18 Birth of Christ c. 4 BC Archelaus 4 BC-AD 6	Death of Pompey 48 Death of Caesar 44 2nd Triumvirate Battle of Philippi 42 Battle of Actium 31 Augustus — First emperor 27 BC-AD 14 **Roman Empire**	**Parthian Empire** Phraates 37-32 Parthians defeat Antony 36
0	Roman governors 6-41 Pontius Pilate 27-37 Death of Christ c. 29 Herod Agrippa I 41-44 Paul's 1st journey, Council at Jerusalem 46/47	Varus defeated in Germany 9 Tiberius 14-37 Gaius (Caligula) 37-41 Claudius 41-54 Conquest of Britain begun 43	Artabanus II 10-40
50 AD	Antonius Felix 52-60 Imprisonment of Paul 58 Porcius Festus 60-62 Paul sent to Rome 60 Gessius Florus 64-66 First Jewish Revolt 66-73 Destruction of Jerusalem 70 Fall of Masada 73 Jewish center at Jamnia	Nero 54-68 1st Persecution of Christians 64 Galba, Otho, Vitellius 68/69 Vespasian 69-79 Titus 79-81 Domitian 81-96 Nerva 96-98 Trajan 98-117	Vologases I 51-80 Parthian War with Rome 53-63 Osroes (Chosroes) 89-128
100 AD **135 AD**	Jewish uprisings in Palestine, Egypt, Mesopotamia 116-117 Bar-Kochba Revolt 132-135 Jerusalem razed, Aelia Capitolina built on site	Campaigns in Dacia 101-107 Hadrian 117-138	Conquest of Nabateans by Romans Trajan invades Parthia 114 Territory lost to Romans regained 118

Herod and His Descendants

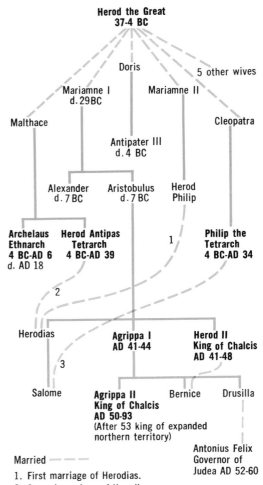

Married - - - -
1. First marriage of Herodias.
2. Second marriage of Herodias.
3. Salome, daughter of Herodias and Herod (sometimes referred to as Philip), danced before Herod Antipas for John the Baptist's head. She married her great-uncle Philip the Tetrarch.

d. died

Roman catapult. A type of artillery used effectively by both Romans and Jews in the battle for Jerusalem, A.D. 69-70.

Gazetteer-Index

This Gazetteer-Index is an alphabetical listing of all geographical names found on the maps of this volume. The spelling of Biblical names used on maps and index is that found in the Revised Standard Version (RSV). Alternative Biblical or other ancient names are given in parentheses. Wherever possible, the modern equivalent (Arabic, Hebrew, Turkish, etc.) of an ancient name is given in italic type. A question mark after the identification of a site indicates that the location is possible or probable but not yet certain. The page numbers of the maps on which the name appears are listed in sequence. The key or grid reference (a letter-figure combination) following the page number(s) refers to the letters and figures at the margins of the maps. For example, Azotus (Ashdod in Old Testament times) [Arabic *Isdud*, Hebrew *Tel Ashdod*] can be found on the maps on pages 23, 25, 26 and 35 at key reference W6 and on page 31 at G8. Entries for locations within or near Jerusalem give the page numbers only for the appropriate Jerusalem maps.

ABBREVIATIONS

T. = Tell, Tel (mound)
Kh. = Khirbet (ruin)
H. = Horvat (ruin)
J. = Jebel (hill or mount)
W. = Wadi (seasonal stream)

A

Abana, *Nahr Barada,* river. 4:Z2
Able, (Abel-beth-maachah), *T. Abil.* 12, 14, 15:Y3; 13:H5
Abel-meholah, *T. Abu Sus.* 15:X5
Abila, *T. Abil,* in Decapolis. 23, 25, 26, 27, 28, 38:Y4
Abila, *T. Abila,* in Abilene. 25, 26:Z2
Abilene, region. 25, 26:X2; 31:H6
Abū Rudays. 39:C6
Abū Zanimah. 39:C6
Abydos, *Arabet el-Madfuneh,* in Egypt. 9, 16:F6
Abydos, *Canakkale,* in Asia Minor. 16:E2
Accaron, *see* Ekron
Acco, (Ptolemais, Acre), *'Akko, T. el-Fukhkhar.* 4, 11, 12, 14, 15, 19, 23, 38:X3; 8:B4; 10:D2; 13:G5
Accrabbah, (Akrabatta), *'Aqraba.* 19:X5
Achaean League. 21, 22:C1
Achaia, Roman province. 32, 33:A1; 36:F3
Achmetha, *see* Ecbatana
Achzib, (Ecdippa), *es-Zib.* 11, 12, 19, 38:X3
Achzib-Acco, region. 19:X3
Acra, in Jerusalem. 22
Adasa, *Kh. 'Addasa.* 23:X6
Adida, (Hadid), *el-Haditheh.* 23, 35:W5
Adora, (Adoraim), *Dura.* 23, 25:W6
Adoraim, (Adora), *Dura.* 12, 15:W6
Adramyttium, *Edremit.* 32, 33:B1; 33:C4
Adria, (Adriatic Sea). 33:A4
Adullam, *T. esh-Sheikh Madhkur.* 11, 12, 15, 19, 23:X6
Aegean Sea. 17, 20, 32, 33:A1
Aenon, spring north of *Kh. Umm el-'Umdan.* 26:X5
Aetolian League. 21, 22:C1
Africa, Roman province. 36:C4
'Afula. 39:D3
Agade, *Abu Ghubar* (?). 9:J4
Agrippias, (Anthedon), *el-Blahiyeh.* 25,26:V6
Agrippina, *Kaukab el-Hawa.* 26, 27:X4
Ahlab, *Kh. el-Mahalib.* 11:X2
Ai, *et-Tell.* 8:B6; 10:E3; 11, 12, 19, 38:X6
Aijalou, *Yalo.* 11, 12, 15:X6
Aijalon, Valley of, *W. Selman.* 4, 11, 12:W6
'Ain el-Qudeirat, (Kadesh-barnea). 38:V8
'Ain Feshkha, spring. 34, 38:X6
'Ain Gedi, (En-gedi). 34, 38:X7
'Ain Ghazzal. 38:Y5

'Ain Karim. 38:X6
'Ajlūn. 39:E3
Akhetaton, *Tell el-Amarna.* 8:E5; 10:A7
Akkad, region. 9:J4
'Akko, (Acco, Ptolemais). 39:D2
Akrabatta, (Accrabbah), *'Aqraba.* 35:X5
Akrabattene, region. 23:X8
Akrabbim, Ascent of, *Naqb es-Safa.* 15:X8
Alaca Huyuk. 9:G1
Alalakh. 9:G3
Al 'Aqabah. 39:D5
Al 'Arīsh. 39:C4
Alashiya, (Cyprus). 9:F3
Aleppo, (Haleb), *Halab.* 16:G3
Alexandria, *Alexandretta,* in Syria. 31:H2
Alexandria, *Gulashkird,* in Carmania. 20:E4
Alexandria, *Iskandariyeh,* in Egypt. 20:B3; 21, 22:D2; 33:66; 37:G5; *see also city plan p. 21*
Alexandria Arachosiorum, *Ghazni.* 20:F3
Alexandria Arion, *Herat.* 20:F3
Alexandria Eschata, *Khodzent.* 21:G2
Alexandrium, *Qarn Sartabeh.* 23, 25, 26:X5
Al Fayyūm. 39:A6
Al Firdān. 39:B4
Al Harmal. 39:E1
Al Karak. 39:E4
Al Khalil, (Hebron). 34:X6
Al Khuraybah. 39:D7
Al Kuntillah. 39:D5
Al Mafraq. 39:E3
Al Mahallah al Kubra. 39:A4
Al Mansūrah. 39:A4
Al Minyā. 39:A7
Al Mudawwarah. 39:E6
Al Qāhirah, (Cairo). 39:A5
Al Qantarah. 39:B4
Al Qatrānah. 39:E4
Al Qunaytirah. 39:E2
Al Qusaymah. 39:D4
Alush, *Wadi el-Esh* (?). 10:C6
Amalek, Amalekites, people. 12:X6; 13:G7; 14:W8
Amanus Mts. 31:H2
Amarna, Tell el-, (Akhetaton). 10, 39:A7
Amastris. 37:G3
Amathus, *T. 'Ammata.* 23, 25, 26:Y5
Amisus. 37:H3
Amman, (Rabba, Philadelphia). 38:Y5; 39:E3
Ammon, region. 4, 11, 12, 14, 15, 19:Z5; 8:C5; 10:E3; 13:H6; 16:G4
Amon, Temple of, *Siwa.* 18, 20:A3
Amorites, people. 8:B6

Amphipolis, *Neochori.* 32, 33:A1
Anab, *Kh. 'Anab es-Saghireh.* 12:W6
Anat, *'Anah.* 16:H4; 17:C3
Anathoth, *Ras el-Kharrubeh.* 12, 19:X6
Anchialus. 37:G3
Ancyra, *Ankara.* 16:F2; 18, 20:B2; 32, 33:C1; 37:G3
Ankuwa, *Alisar Huyuk.* 9:G2
An Nakhl. 39:D5
Anthedon, (Agrippias), *el-Blahiyeh.* 23, 25:V6
Antigonid Kingdom. 21, 22:C1
Anti-Lebanon, mts. 4:Y2; 8:C2; 31:J5
Antioch, *Antakya,* in Syria. 22:D1; 31:H3; 32, 33:D2; 37:H4; *see also city plan p. 30*
Antioch, *Yalvac,* in Pisidia. 32:C1; 32:C2; 37:G3
Antipatris, (Aphek), *Ras el-'Ain.* 25, 26, 28, 35, 38:W5
Antium, *Anzio.* 36:D3
Antonia Fortress, in Jerusalem. 25, 29, 34
Apamea, *Qal'at el-Mudiq.* 31, 37:H4
Aphairema, (Ephraim, Ophrah), *et-Taiyibeh* (?). 23:X5
Aphek, (Antipatris), *Ras el- 'Ain.* 10:D3; 11, 12, 14, 15, 38:X5
Aphek, *Fiq,* in Transjordan. 15:Y4
Aphek, *T. Kurdaneh,* in Asher. 11, 12:X3
Apollonia, *Arsuf,* in Palestine. 19, 23, 25, 26, 35:W5
Apollonia, *Pollinia,* in Macedonia. 32, 33:A1
Apollonia, *Sozopol,* on Black Sea. 18:B1
Appius, Forum of, (Appi Forum). 33:A4
Aqaba, Gulf of. 10, 39:D6
Ar, *el-Misna'.* 14, 15:Y7
Arabah, *el-Ghor, Wadi al 'Arabah.* 4, 15:X8; 10:D5; 13:H8; 39:E4
Arabia, region. 9:H5; 18, 20:C3; 21, 22:E2; 37:J5
Arabian Sea. 21:F4
Arabs, people. 16:H5; 17:C3
Arachosia, region. 18, 20:F3
Arad, (Great Arad), *T. 'Arad.* 8:B7; 10:D4; 11, 12, 14, 15, 23, 34, 38:X7; 13:G6; 39:D3
Arad of Beth-yeroham, *T. el-Milh.* 15, 38:X7
Aral Sea. 17, 18, 20:E1
Aram, (Syria), region. 14, 15:Y2
Aram-Damascus, region. 13:H4
Arameans, people. 11:Y2
Aram-zobah, region. 13:J4
Araq, el-Emir, (Tyrus). 38:Y6
Ararat, (Urartu), region. 16:H2
Ararat, Mt., *Buyuk Agri Dagi.* 9, 16:J2

Araxes, river. 9:K2; 16:J2; 18:D1
Arbela, *Erbil,* in Assyria. 9, 16:J3; 18, 20:D2
Arbela, *Irbid,* in Decapolis. 26:Y4
Arbela, *Kh. Irbid,* in Galilee. 23:X4
Archelais, *Kh. 'Auja et-Tahta.* 26:X5
Ardus, (Arvad), *Erwad, Ruwad.* 31:H4
Areopolis, (Rabbath-moab), *Kh. er-Rabba.* 26, 28:Y7
Argob, region. 13:H5; 14:Y3
Aria, region. 18, 21:F3
Aribi, (Arabs), people. 16:H4
Ariha, (Jericho). 34:X6
Arimathea, (Ramathaim), *Rentis.* 26:X5
'Arish, Wadi al-, (River of Egypt). 4:V8; 39:C5
Armenia, region. 18, 20:C2; 21, 22:E1; 37:J3
Arnon, *W. al-Mawjib,* river. 4, 11, 12, 14, 15, 19, 23, 25, 26, 35:Y7; 8:B6; 10:E4
Aroer, *'Ara'ir,* in Moab. 11, 12, 38:Y6; 13:H6
Arpad, *T. Erfad.* 16:G3
Arvad, (Ardus), *Erwad, Ruwad.* 9, 16:G3; 13:H3; 18:C3; 31:H4
Arzawa, region. 8:E2
Ascalon, (Ashkelon), *'Ashqelon.* 23, 25, 26, 35, 38:W6
Ashdod, (Azotus), *Isdud, T. Ashdod.* 8:A6; 11, 12, 14, 15, 19, 23, 38:W6; 10, 39:D3
Ashdod, region. 19:W6
Ashdod Yam. 38:W6
Asher, tribe. 11, 12:X3
Ashkelon, (Ascalon), *'Ashqelon.* 8:A6; 10:D3; 11, 12, 14, 15, 19, 23, 38:W6; 13:G6
'Ashqelon. 39:D3
Ashtaroth, *T. 'Ashtarah.* 8:C4; 10:E2; 11, 12, 14, 15:Y4; 13:H5
Asia, Roman province. 32, 33:B1; 33:C5; 37:G3
Asia Minor, region. 20:B2
Asochis, *Kh. el-Lon.* 26, 27:X4
Asphaltitis, Lake, (Dead Sea). 25, 26, 35:X6
As Salt. 39:E3
As Samu', (Eshtemoa). 34:X7
Asshur, *Qal'at Sherqat.* 9:J3; 16:J3; 18:C2
Assos, *Behramkoy.* 33:B1
Assuwa, region. 8:E1
Assyria, region. 9:J3; 16:H3; 17:C2
Assyriau Empire. 16:G4
Astacus. 16:F2
Astorga. 36:A2
Ataroth, *Kh. Attarus.* 15:Y6
Athens. 17, 18, 20, 32, 33:A2; 21, 22:C1; 36:F4
'Atlit, (Pilgrims Castle). 38:W4
Attalia, *Antalya.* 32:C2

47

Picture Credits

The editor and publisher wish to express their thanks and appreciation to the following for supplying illustrations:

The American Numismatic Society, New York: pages 20 (bottom), 21 (top right), 22 (center left), 28 (bottom right), 29 (bottom left), 35 (bottom right). Henry Angelo-Castrillon: page 32 (top right), 36 (right). The Bettmann Archive, New York: page 42. The Trustees of the British Museum: pages 16 (all three photos), 18 (top). Ernest J. Dupuy: pages 32 (top left), 36 (center), 37 (center). GAF Pana-Vue Slides: pages 24 (top), 28 (top). Hebrew University, Jerusalem, Department of Archaeology: page 22 (bottom right). Iran National Tourist Office, New York: page 18 (left). Israel Government Tourist Office, New York: title page, pages 5 (bottom left), 11 (top), 27 (left), 29 (top left), 30 (second from top), 35 (two photos at top). The Israel Museum, Jerusalem: pages 11 (top right), 14 (top right), 18 (bottom right), 28 (bottom left). Istanbul Museum: page 30 (top). Italian Government Travel Office: page 36 (left). Nancy L. Lapp: page 12. From Lepsius, *Denkmaeler*: page 10 (right). Herbert G. May: page 27 (bottom right). The Metropolitan Museum of Art: pages 2, 22 (top left and top right), 37 (bottom right). Museo Nazionale, Naples: pages 20 (top), 21 (center right). Museum of Fine Arts, Boston: page 24 (bottom). Notre Dame de Sion, Jerusalem: page 29 (center bottom). The Oriental Institute, University of Chicago: pages 17, 38 (center). The University Museum, University of Pennsylvania: pages 9, 37 (left). Wide World Photos: page 30 (third from top).

Photographs from collection of Professor Harry Thomas Frank: pages 5 (three photos at right), 7 (both), 8, 10 (left), 11 (bottom), 14 (top left), 21 (top left), 22 (center right and bottom left), 25, 27 (center and top right), 29 (center top and right), 30 (bottom), 35 (bottom left), 38 (top two photos and bottom photo).